75° AA

THE THEORY OF
MORAL INCENTIVES
IN CUBA

THE THEORY OF
MORAL INCENTIVES
IN CUBA

by

Robert M. Bernardo

Introduction by Irving Louis Horowitz

THE UNIVERSITY OF ALABAMA PRESS

University, Alabama

FOR BEVERLY

Contents

Preface

The main thrust of this work relates to the capacity of moral or nonmonetary incentives to replace the market in the specific Cuban context. To some extent it applies to China, too, and perhaps even to North Korea, the three countries in the socialist world that have most forcefully championed the cause of nonmonetary egalitarian means of modernization. In this contribution to the current discussion on moral versus material monetary incentives, I shall contrast the use of nonmonetary (moral) means to the monetary wages system and show its equivalence to the communist equalitarian rule of "from each according to his ability, to each according to his need." I shall show in what practical, but not logical, sense this implies the elimination of the market wages system of labor allocation including motivation. The Cuban and Chinese view of the debate on incentives is that the test of whether a society relies primarily on moral incentives is found in the extent to which it has abolished the market wages system—where labor is allocated like any other commodity. Since late 1966, both countries may be said to have eliminated the labor market in an important practical sense of the word "market."

I deal with the mechanism of moral incentives as a resource allocation system alternative to the market organizing

vii

principle. Ideally, that mechanism is viewed by classical Marx-ists as a decentralist version of the centrally administrative mode of production; the mechanism of moral incentives is seen as a partial substitute for the centrally administrative prin-ciple of organizing modern complex societies. This point is related to another made in this book—that the Guevaraists were really decentralists at heart. There are quotations in sup-port of the opposite view—that they were ultra-centralists. But the latter seems like a caricature of the Guevaraist view. Dr. Ernesto "Che" Guevara introduced and championed the cause of moral incentives in Cuba and argued for mathematical methods to decentralize and simplify the tasks of administra-tive planning. The Guevaraists argued that moral incentives, ideally, is a nonmarket decentralist process, an organizational building-block based on feelings of group solidarity. By un-leashing a cultural revolution of immensely profound dimen-sions, Cuban and Chinese policymakers hoped to reconcile managerial and worker interests with the community's as out-lined by the leaders, thus cutting down on the need for de-tailed instructions and supervision and avoiding the evils of bureaucracy. In contrast to this, many Eastern European coun-tries have opted for the Libermanist alternative of partially decentralizing the administrative system. By Libermanist is meant a system where the principal goal of the firm on which material incentives depend is profits or sales or a mixture of both. The definition implies the use of the highly unequal salaries and bonuses of the market method of recruitment and motivation. The Cuban and Chinese leaders consider Liber-manism as capitalism of a peculiar kind and set their common solution as a viable alternative. Barry Richman, whose field work on Chinese and Soviet management is cited here, states that the former achieved greater decentralization than the latter, at least up to 1966. Franz Schurmann's work on China, as well as Ezra Vogel's, seems to indicate a similar obser-vation. Richman and Vogel give much of the credit for this decentralization to the heavy use made of the vehicles for deepening and implementing the mechanism of moral incentives. While the few and often patchy works in the area of moral incentives in Cuba and China deal with it either as a socio-psychological and a type of political compliance system, or mainly as a motivator complementary to material incentives in given places of production, I discuss it as a device for allocating scarce material resources to their competing uses. I also inquire into the efficiency of this non-wage system from the point of view of the current optimal allocation of resources and from the point of view of development strategy. Finally I discuss the historical conditions under which the mechanism of moral incentives has flourished in Cuba—and in China and North Korea by implication—and go into the likelihood of preserving the system in the future.

A claim I shall be making is that Cuba has become the first country in the world to have achieved communism under conditions of relative peace. I do not mean that it has achieved affluence, nor do I mean that it is a fully functioning mature communist society, nor that it is democratic. I mean it simply in the organizational and allocative sense of the word, in the sense in which Soviet War Communism in the early history of the Soviet Union seemed to conform to a communist organizational model. I mean mainly that it is the first to institutionalize the communist or egalitarian rule of production and distribution. One might reply, in objection to this view, that commune property, not state property, is the professed ideal form of property under communism, particularly in agriculture. This is legally not the case in Cuba where some thirty percent of agricultural lands are "owned privately" by small farmers. However, we are less interested in merely juridical definitions than in effective ownership systems. Moreover, one cannot strictly separate the allocative and ownership points of view in defining a form of productive organization, for the nature of the allocative rules determines the real character of ownership. For example, the Cuban private sector in agriculture remains private in name only; in reality they are subject to centralized planning and share in communal activities like the state enterprises. In suggesting the view that Cuban socialism has become communism, I am not claiming more than what the Cuban leaders assert or imply. Since late 1966, the policy has been "the parallel construction of socialism and communism." The nonmonetary egalitarian rule has been achieved, however, in the general framework of a semi-militarized society at holy war with underdevelopment.

Chapter one offers evidence to suggest that, by the time they took over the government, the radical intellectuals who led the revolution identified with a variant of Marxism we might call classical. The chief elements of the latter are its anti-capitalist, anti-market, and equalitarian stress and its theory of alienation. The alienation of man from his true or ethically desirable community-centered nature, the theory held, is chiefly due to the market and its companion institutions of competition for money, private or saleable property, and the like.

Chapter two discusses a little known area—the structure of the Cuban firm—under moral incentives. It follows naturally from the first chapter's treatment of the major controversy over the choice of systems during the formative years of socialism, for that debate was really over the desirable mix between moral and material incentives in the organization of the firm. Chapter three continues this inquiry into the mechanism of moral incentives as it operates in the more important field of labor organization. Chapter four then examines the efficiency of moral incentives, an investigation that leads to the important question of what happened to the Cuban gross national product in the past eleven years or so. A thorough discussion of the latter dimension of performance is needed to answer the question of whether departures from efficient allocation under moral incentives, if any, might have been over-compensated by sheer gains in the volume of national income associated with successes in raising the supply of effort through the use of moral incentives. That discussion, in turn, leads to the topic of chapter five—the historical viability of moral incentives as a resource allocating system. Surely, a crucial consideration on the future of moral incentives in Cuba and China is the system's ability to increase the growth rate of their respective national incomes.

In writing the empirical part of this book on Cuba, I was concerned about its permanent value and long-term relevance because of the dynamic character of Cuban institutions. Innovations are constantly in progress; reforms in the planning administration are many; experiments are forever being tried; an institution now being set up may be torn down tomorrow. By the time a thorough study is completed, it is rendered out of date by the relentless march of current and future events. Such was the fate, for instance, of my doctoral dissertation on Central Planning procedures in Cuba which I wrote for the University of California at Berkeley in 1967. In revising and updating that work several times, I realized the futility of keeping up with the historical march of new knowledge about Cuban society. I decided to write it again but this time with the more limited aim of capturing the essence of the dramatic social changes spanning the years 1959 to 1970. Thus could the future still find my study of lasting relevance, if I gave it this historical perspective. I then decided to remove many sections of the old work of merely transitory value, or which had been chronicled in detail elsewhere, and sought a nail, so to speak, from which to hang a somewhat abstract picture of the first twelve years of the Cuban Revolution. I found this historical focus in the grand controversy which raged in Cuba right at the very start of its socialist experiment, and which hinged on the crucial issue of the desirable mix between moral incentives and material ones, both in the organization of the firm and of labor. The result was a new work only partially related to the revised version of my dissertation.

I should now like to say something about my sources of information; for the kind of project I had in mind, I found our original and official sources in North America more than adequate, although these are widely scattered and disparate. In regard to more comprehensive and detailed facts and statistics on planning and national income, on which my project did not crucially depend, these are only partially available anywhere owing to some secrecy on the part of the main planners or to their absence, particularly in the early years of Cuban socialism. The best source of statistics we have, the *Boletín Estadístico de Cuba, 1962–1966* and the *Compendio Estadístico de Cuba, 1965–1968* have to be painstakingly reworked for reliability and comparability to our standard definitions of national income, and they are not comprehensive nor are their procedures explained. On the question of secrecy, Dudley Seers and his associates, as far back as 1962, related their failure to penetrate through the statistics kept by the Central Planning Board, as they tell us in their well-known book on Cuba written at about that time; but their lack of success was also due to the lack then of a statistical annual. Michael Frayn, who covered the tenth anniversary of the Cuban Revolution for the London Observer, reported the unwillingness of the Central Planning Board to give him specific data on labor organization. Even the recent works of such well-placed field observers as Edward Boorstein, Paul Sweezy, Leo Huberman, and Maurice Zeitlin failed to yield new statistics not already available to the academic researcher in North America.

Since Cuba initiated its own "great leap forward" and "cultural revolution" in late 1966, our sources of information have progressively dwindled. A significant number of periodical sources, including some of the best journals such as

Cuba Socialista and *Nuestra Industria: Revista Económica*, were discontinued at this time. The Official Gazette or *Gaceta Oficial* still appears in print, but its export has been banned by the Cuban government. For data after 1967 I was thus forced to rely heavily on the weekly reviews in English of the party newspaper *Granma* and the monthly *Cuba Economic News* as well as the field research of recent visitors to Cuba.

My interest in Cuba began at Stanford when I took some courses under Professors Sweezy and Baran; Professor Ronald Hilton then gave me an encouraging opinion when he was still editing *Hispanic American Report* that I would not unearth very much more data pertinent to my study than I would by digging for sources at the Stanford libraries. Early in 1969 an informal evening spent at the University of Guelph with the Cuban consul from Toronto led me to tap his consulate for pamphlets and other recent periodical materials. Conversations with members of the Venceremos Brigade at Berkeley and the many documentaries I saw there and in the greater Toronto area gave me, I hope, a vicarious experience and appreciation of the Cuban situation. At Berkeley, I owe a great debt to Professors Gregory Grossman and Benjamin Ward for their encouragement and detailed supervision of my doctoral dissertation, on which this book is partly based. My third supervisor, Franz Schurmann, helped stir my interest in organizational and ideological comparisons with China and related some of his first-hand impressions of Cuba. Grant Barnes of the University of California Press gave me the initial encouragement to write this book several years ago and gave me generous criticism which I used as a starting point. Daniel Fusfield of the University of Michigan read a primitive version of the manuscript and gave me a useful criticism. Irving Louis Horowitz commented on an early version of a large portion of this work. My editors at UAP improved my presentation and gave perceptive comments. I thank Dr. Eric Baklanoff, the Director of International Programs at the University of Alabama for sponsoring this book, and making it possible to appear earlier in print. I also owe great debt to our leading scholar in the field of Cuban studies, Dr. Carmelo Mesa-Lago of the University of Pittsburgh, who read the manuscript in detail and corrected it for errors. His works on Cuban labor are the pioneering efforts in the area of moral incentives in Cuba; these as well as our extensive correspondence were a mine of information and insight. John Skinner, Dean of Social Science at the University of Guelph, also made it possible for me to write this book by his encouragement—backed by his offer of good working conditions. I also benefited from a fruitful semester in 1970 as a research associate in the faculty seminar and Project on the Comparative Study of Communism at the University of California. None of the above persons should be blamed for errors which might still remain.

Berkeley, California   ROBERT M. BERNARDO
January, 1971

Introduction

The Marxist theory of False Consciousness declares that revolutions often fail to materialize as a result of inaccurate and inept appraisals of the nature of the social system. In our age, when so many revolutions are made and fail in the name of Marxian Socialism, it might be well to amend this doctrine of False Consciousness by pointing out that those who bring about a revolution oftentimes make inaccurate and even inept appraisals of the very nature of the social revolution that they have brought into existence. Those who with sharp eyes and pure hearts make a revolution are not infrequently the very same people who falsify the terms of that revolution. Ironically, they often do so under the assumption—or rather the presumption—that their own sharp eyes and pure hearts somehow can be substituted for the vagaries of society as a whole. In less poetic terms, those who make the revolution may be the ones who break the revolution.

What stimulates this observation is this outstanding study of moral and economic incentives in the Cuban social systems since the Castro revolution. Professor Bernardo focuses upon the role of ideology and morality in driving Cuban economic planners toward fundamentally negative decisions about the nature of market relationships, decisions that in turn have led to a series of problems which seem to presage yet a higher series of catastrophe.

Since Professor Bernardo has ably summarized the substance of his volume on *The Theory of Moral Incentives in Cuba* in his preface, I should like to address myself to the main problem discussed in the text: The place of moral incentives in stimulating economic growth. Perhaps the question can be summarized as follows: Can a society have moral incentives under conditions of economic scarcity? More specifically, can a single crop economy be designated as socialist in any but the most desultory sense? In a broader context, is it not the case that the Cuban emphasis on moral incentives not only violates classical economic rules concerning the market determination of prices and profits, but even the Marxist notion of the labor theory of value?

From my own point of view, and without in any way minimizing the enormous achievement of Professor Bernardo, the problem may be one of causation rather than ideology. That is to say, the Marxist theory of moral incentives to labor presupposes the solution of problems of material incentives. Only when the ego needs are fully gratified, only when a material abundance is available for all to share in, does the Marxist doctrine of moral incentives come into play. In effect, the neo-Marxist—what Professor Bernardo calls Guevaraist —doctrine moves up the timetable of economic development; that is, it accelerates the doctrine of moral incentives so that the reasons for effort and labor are connected to the political survival of the system, rather than the economic abundance created by that system.

In some strange way, the Cuban economy has responded to the role of political ideology by noting that the essence of planning is not so much economic growth as it is political mobilization. And in this sense, the theory of moral incentives has had a binding value on Cuban society far in excess of any economic profitability or losses occasioned by the premature disavowal of market incentives to labor.

One might say that the Cuban economy has taken an enormous gamble by assuming that there would be enough nonmaterial incentives to maintain a stable state within the economy. Whether this is so or not of course depends not only on the state of mind of the Cuban working class, but the levels of production and consumption of Cuban society as a whole. Obviously, if the question of economic incentives were one of simply monetary purchasing power, unemployment rates, absenteeism, and even labor sabotage would be considerably higher than in fact they are. But how long can a society substitute moral fervor for consumer satisfaction? The Christian-Marxist doctrine of men living not by bread alone ignores the fact that there is an intermediate stage between matter and morals—what might be called comfort and well being. Here is where the vital trade-off between economy and morality takes place. Whether or not Cuban society can sustain fervor for the regime sufficient to permit the continued growth of the GNP at the expense of consumer fulfillment is extremely difficult and hazardous to predict.

Professor Bernardo's findings might best be evaluated by taking a balance-sheet view of the situation. The moral economy has succeeded in achieving a high degree of egalitarianism as a by-product of Cuban productive organization, and there can be no doubt that Professor Bernardo is correct in observing that this was achieved largely by the use of the allocation system of moral stimulation. It is also clear that the price of this egalitarianism is a high demand for material goods—and the choice is select among those goods.

It is also true that the theory of moral stimulation alters old relationships and ends the exaggerated separation of supply and demand for money and goods. Wage differentials are reduced, price differentials are reduced, leisure and labor are flattened out, and in general, there is a definite complementarity between moral and material incentives in such a system. But again, the problem here is whether in fact there are such things as moral incentives, or whether the doctrine is not simply a disguised way of defining unpaid labor time, or labor time paid at reduced wages for the purposes of increasing the gross national product.

One might take an orthodox rather than a revisionist Marxian view and claim that common sense dictates that we should average in unpaid labor time with paid labor time to arrive at the actual earning power of Cuban labor. Or that, in point of fact, the theory of moral incentives is a way of maintaining a socialist economy in a single crop situation with a minimal amount of inflationary spiraling and pressures for trade union reform.

A virtue of the book is that it is written without an ideological axe to grind, and without the usual passions accompanying almost all books on the subject of socialist Cuba. A further virtue of the book is that Professor Bernardo etches out in great detail, and at times with considerable eloquence, the way in which problems of economics become, in effect, problems of ethics. Perhaps the question left unanswered by the author, and the one that can only be resolved with time, is whether good leadership might accelerate the stages of economic growth in Cuba and might even permit stage skipping. And beyond that, whether a charismatic political structure, such as that which obtains in Cuba, can actually reverse the historical process and create a moral economy based on a new socialist man, under conditions of relative economic scarcity.

The anomaly is that Cuban leaders, whether they be Guevara or Castro, have in effect spiritualized problems of economic production and allocation. They seem to be the first true idealists to emanate from the Marxist-Socialist tradition. Perhaps this philosophical outcome should not have been unexpected, since the Cuban revolution always seemed to be a matter of will and a problem in decision theory, rather than a matter of determinism or a matter of history. In a sense the post-revolutionary Cuban leadership has carried forth this volitional or idealistic theory of the revolution and has made the success of the socialist economy also a matter of will, which of course ultimately involves questions of moral choice. Thus it is that the book by Bernardo provides a fascinating episode not just in the annals of political economy but, even more profoundly, in political sociology: The way in which problems of political leadership and social class determine the struggle of society and, ultimately, the structure of values which provide the ideological fuel for that society. By taking just a small problem, Professor Bernardo has illuminated the entire ecstasy and agony of the Cuban revolution and perhaps of world socialism in our times.

IRVING LOUIS HOROWITZ

Rutgers University
May 5, 1971.

We are constructing . . . a somewhat different formula than the
ones used in other socialist countries
. . . moral stimulation.

> Ernesto "Che" Guevara, 1962

And yet I have seen it inspire men
to effort, kept going and spurred
on by the possibility of earning a
banner. Does this not constitute an
interesting topic?

> Armando Hart Dávalos, member
> of the Political Bureau
> at Havana University, 1969

The Revolution aspires to equalize
incomes, from the bottom up . . .
regardless of the type of work . . . .
This principle will surely be given
a name by "learned", "experienced"
economists . . . who will claim this
goes against the laws of economics.
The question is which economics?

> Fidel Castro, July 26, 1969

We, the leaders of the Revolution,
have cost the people too much in
our process of learning.

> Fidel Castro, July 26, 1970

CHAPTER ONE

Choice Among Several Systems
in the Formative Years
of Cuban Socialism

The Shaping Influence of Guevaraist Ideology

In his latest work on Cuba, Herbert Matthews unduly stresses the shaping influence of Fidel Castro's personality on the Cuban Revolution.[1] Yet the ideological role of Dr. Ernesto "Che" Guevara seems to have been as equally important if not more so; he was Cuba's leading theoretician and planner during the formative years of Cuban socialism. In that commanding position, he exerted the sheer force of his will which, after his departure from Cuba, transformed Cuban socialism into its higher stage—communism of an austere kind surpassing Soviet War Communism or even China in the era of the post-cultural revolution.

I shall argue that the leading Cuban revolutionary intellectuals possessed a classical (anti-market) ideology which influenced their choice of organizational means. The psychological theory of rationalization suggests, of course, that ideology may have been a cover-up for the expedient policies and power plays of a person or group. For example, the equalitarian and technological elements of Marxism may have been

1. See his book, *Fidel Castro* (New York: Simon and Schuster, 1969).

3

merely espoused to provide legitimacy for the leadership in their take-over of power. But the facts indicate that whether or not they were genuine ideals or expedient ones, the main Cuban leadership seems to have implemented some of their organizational reforms under the influence of a set of values they were eager to actualize and to which they were committed by their classical Marxist ideology. Moreover, whether or not ideology did in fact influence the choice of both goals and means is to be determined by the particular facts of a given historical situation. Due to the inscrutability of the main leaders—since we cannot enter their minds—one can only infer the plausibility of our thesis by examining their public words and, more importantly, their deeds.

Derived Preference for Administrative Socialism

Before going further, however, a popular hypothesis on the origins of socialism in Cuba needs to be dealt with. This is the Sartre-Baran challenge-and-response theory which holds that the main leaders possessed no initial socialist ideology; instead they were humanists who set themselves the task of doing, in an experimental manner, what needed to be done.[2] This "muddling through" eventually led to their discovery and espousal of Marxist socialism. Paul Baran described this theory thus:

> Nor was it before the unilateral abrogation of the Cuban sugar quota by the American government, that further American enterprises were taken over. And it was not until the recent general embargo on most United States exports to Cuba that . . . the fledgling Cuban Revolution [was] . . . pushed . . . in the direction of economic planning and socialism.[3]

2. Jean Paul Sartre, *Sartre on Cuba* (New York: Ballantine Books, 1961), p. 80. The same point was made by Paul Sweezy and Leo Huberman in "Cuba: Anatomy of a Revolution," *Monthly Review*, July–August, 1960, p. 146.

3. Paul A. Baran, "Reflections on the Cuban Revolution," *Monthly Review*, February, 1961, p. 520.

Guevara described the hypothesis above by claiming that the main leaders, by a process of groping and trial and error found reality to be Marxist. Current scholarship now regards the "blow-counterblow" view as hasty and a biased account by persons eager to prove Marxian social theory and who were themselves Marxist. In his interview with the journalist Lee Lockwood, Castro owned to being a "utopian socialist" of long-standing; he admitted that for political strategic reasons, he and the other leaders kept their socialist plans to themselves. Castro's early "utopian socialism", as he described it, was an anti-market [classical] Marxism that offered general aims and means for the radical transformation of Cuban society.⁴ Almost as much was similarly admitted by Fidel Castro in his interview earlier with Herbert Matthews. He was, according to this interview, a "utopian Marxist" by July 26, 1953, and a Marxist-Leninist by mid-1960.⁵ In his interview with Lockwood, Castro admitted being a "utopian Marxist" since his last years in the University of Havana and had then begun "to think of different forms of the organization of production and of property although in a completely idealistic way, without any scientific basis. You might say that I had begun to transform myself into a kind of utopian socialist." ⁶ There is no controversy regarding the Marxism of the other leaders of the Revolution. Although there is doubt concerning the solidity of the Marxist background of its leaders as a whole, Ernesto "Che" Guevara, Raúl Castro, Osvaldo Dorticós, Antonio Núñez Jiménez and Alfredo Guevara were radicals whose Marxism antedated their assumption of power on the first day of 1959.

Fidel Castro in the two interviews cited may have been

4. "Interview: Fidel Castro," *Playboy*, January, 1967, pp. 64, 67.
5. As quoted in Herbert L. Matthews, "Return to Cuba," *Hispanic American Review* (HAR), Special Issue, Stanford University, 1964, p. 11.
6. Ibid., pp. 62–63.

projecting his utopian Marxism retroactively. The actual behavior of the Cuban central planners, however, is consistent with his words. By the end of May 1960, some five months before the declaration of the United States embargo (and its accompanying wave of nationalization) in October of the same year, Cuba had passed the benchmark for classifying it as an administrative socialist system. The "commanding heights" in the production system had been formally nationalized or else large private firms were "intervened" by the government and managed according to the administrative method. In agriculture and industry, private ownership was still more widespread than state ownership. However, state administrative intervention of the private sector was extensive; the cumulative fixing of prices and quantity regulations issued increasingly since mid-1959 had effectively paralyzed the market system by early 1960. Most serious observers of Cuban reality date the installment of socialism in Cuba as falling between March and May of 1960 [7]—about six to seven months before the United States declared its embargo.

In an article he wrote with refreshing candor, Guevara reminisced on the rapid transformation into comprehensive nonmarket socialism: ". . . the most momentous acts of the first year were the Agrarian Reform and the takeover of the National Banks. . . . [which] led. . . . to new forms of organization which were more equitable and proper." With respect to the Department of Industrialization created in November, 1959 and which he headed,

> it was conceived in order to realize great tasks . . . to develop industry based on the substitution of imported products of

7. These dates are given and justified, for example, by Leo Huberman and Paul Sweezy in their *Cuba, The Anatomy of a Revolution* (New York: Monthly Review Press, 1960); and also by James O'Connor in his "Industrial Organization in the Old and New Cubas," *Science and Society*, Spring, 1966, pp. 180–181, *et passim*.

a simple technology. A list of the imported products was
taken . . . . the most important ones in the foreign trade
records . . . . [and] the search for offers began.[8]

He continued that the process above culminated "during
all of 1960. . . . with the [February] visit of Vice-Prime
Minister Mikoyan of the Soviet Union. The socialist countries
sent their representatives to Cuba and credit agreements were
signed for the building of a great number of basic industries."
Promises were obtained for a steel industry, electric plants, an
oil refinery, and a geological survey from the Soviet Union;
an automobile factory from Czechoslovakia; $60 million for
24 different plants from China; 15 plants from Rumania; 5
plants from Bulgaria; 12 plants from Poland; and for 10 plants
from East Germany.[9]

When the American trade embargo came in October
1960, the Cuban leaders were not very surprised or upset since
they expected the United States to take hostile action to stop
the movement towards a socialist transformation. The shift to
the Eastern bloc countries would be disruptive, but was faced
squarely and regarded as a minor cost to pay for a nationalist
and comprehensive socialist system.

The Guevaraists argued that Cuba was a small country
with a developed communications system which made it relatively easy to plan centrally. They argued rather simplistically
—since most programmers doubt it—that mathematical programming of resources would make comprehensive centralized
planning practicable: ". . . modern planning methods will
assume their importance, and it will become possible to approximate the ideal of managing the economy by means of

8. For these quotes, see Ernesto Che Guevara, "Tareas industriales de la Revolución en los años venideros," *Cuba Socialista*, March
1962, pp. 29–31.
9. Ibid., p. 30. In 1958 a dollar was equal to a Cuban peso. I shall
use this equation throughout this study since the Cubans still do.

mathematical analysis . . . . The different branches of production will be made more automatic . . . ."[10]

Like other classical socialists and Marxists, the Guevaraists affirmed the adequacy of a physical approach to resource planning: and therefore they denied the law of value (pricing laws of the market).

> We deny the possibility of the conscious use of the Law of Value . . . the category of commodity (*mercancía*) in the relation between state enterprises, and we consider all these establishments as parts of a single integrated enterprise which is the State . . . . The Law of Value and the plan are two mutually contradictory terms . . . centralized planning is the mode of being of socialist society, its definitive category . . .[11]

This view is identical to a view expressed once by Paul Sweezy (and other classical Marxists such as Preobrazhenski and Bukharin):

> . . . value loses its relevance [under socialism] and importance; its place is taken by the principle of planning . . . . Value and planning are as much opposed, and for the same reasons, as capitalism and socialism.[12]

In regard to the choice of an incentive system, Guevara showed an anti-Libermanist position in December 1962 (as he did with René Dumont in August 1960):

> Cuba always stresses the ideological aspect, the education of the minds of the people, and the call to duty . . . . Then comes the necessary material stimulation to mobilize the people.[13]

The same thoughts were expressed a year later: "For me, it is a question of doctrine. Economic socialism without communist

10. Ernesto Che Guevara, "La banca, el crédito y el socialismo," *Cuba Socialista*, March, 1964, p. 36.

11. Ibid.

12. Paul Sweezy, *Theory of Capitalist Development* (New York: Monthly Review Press, 1956), pp. 53–54.

13. As quoted in *HAR*, February, 1963, p. 1104.

morality does not interest me." He added: "We are struggling against poverty, but at the same time against alienation. One of the fundamental objectives of Marxism is to eliminate interest—the factor of 'individual interest'—and profit from psychological motivations." [14] In the Spring of 1965, shortly before his final departure from Cuba, Guevara repeated the same thoughts, which were reminiscent of the 1962 Chinese Socialist Education Campaign that several years later burst into the Great Cultural Revolution:

> . . . no subterfuge is needed. It is carried on by the state's educational apparatus, as a function of general, technical, and ideological, culture through such agencies as the Ministry of Education and the Party's information apparatus. Education takes hold of the masses and the new attitude tends to become a habit; the masses continue to absorb it and to influence those who have not yet educated themselves.[15]

Guevara's views recall Sweezy's again:

> The new generation [Yugoslav]—its mentality and attitudes have been and are being shaped by an economic system in which the goals and initiative of the individual are indistinguishable from those of capitalism. The types produced by such an environment range from the philistine through the unprincipled opportunist to the greedy corruptionist.
>
> . . . .
>
> It is necessary not only to abolish private property in the interest of production, but also production for profit. Beware of the Market; it is capitalism's secret weapon! Comprehensive planning is the heart and core of genuine socialism! [16]

14. *L'Express* (Paris), July 25, 1963, as quoted in Theodore Draper, *Castroism: Theory and Practice* (Praeger, 1965), p. 159.

15. Ernesto Che Guevara, "Notes on Socialism and Man," *International Socialist Review*, Winter, 1966, p. 20.

16. For this quote and other similarities with Guevara, see Leo Huberman and Paul Sweezy, "The Peaceful Transition from Socialism to Capitalism," *Monthly Review*, March, 1964.

The last quotation raises the plausibility that North American Marxism may have exerted a significant ideological contribution during the formative years of Cuban socialism. A great number of Western Hemisphere Marxist theoreticians and technicians found an exciting experimental social laboratory in Cuba during the latter half of 1959 and particularly in early 1960, soon after a revitalized central planning board (JUCEPLAN) was created in February of that year. Their influence seems to have been felt by the Cuban planners. The classical school of Marxism identified with Baran, Sweezy and Huberman in America was strikingly identical with Guevara's. In March, 1960 Leo Huberman and Paul Sweezy spent three weeks in Cuba and gave a conference on national planning. This was attended by high-ranking Cuban officials, the most notable of whom were Guevara and Antonio Núñez Jiménez (Executive Director of INRA *), the two most influential planners in Cuba at this early period. The content of this conference was later serialized in the April 5, 6, 7, and 8, 1960, issues of *Revolución*. In these talks Professor Sweezy reiterated the classical Marxian doctrines of the instability of a semi-socialist solution (since the larger remaining private sector would presumably sabotage such an arrangement), the corrupting properties of private ownership and of the market-material incentive system. Like the other classical Marxist consultants, he also stressed the need for comprehensive administrative planning.

On their second three-week trip to Cuba in September and October, 1960 Professor Baran accompanied Huberman and Sweezy.[17] Baran's book, *Political Economy of Growth*, popular among Latin American leftists, urged the need for an

* Instituto Nacional de la Reforma Agraria (National Institute of Agrarian Reform).

17. This visit formed the basis of his "Reflections on the Cuban Revolution," serialized in the January and February 1961 issues of *Monthly Review*.

administrative big-push of the Soviet kind. Guevara is known to have read it and a friendship developed between him and Baran evidenced by Guevara's commemorative note in Baran's *A Collective Portrait* (1965). In addition, there was a heavy influence of Latin American Marxist planners, such as Juan Noyola from Mexico and Chilean Marxian social planners and technicians. These were active and dominated the administrative staff of INRA from the second half of 1959 giving instructions on planning based on translations of orthodox Soviet and Czech planning manuals.[18]

The fact is that there were capitalist and socialist organizational alternatives proposed by different groups of Cuban planners and their foreign consultants during the formative years of Cuban socialism. The consideration of these several systems indeed constituted the great debate which has been incorrectly dated as occurring from 1963 to 1965.[19] This controversy, in contrast to, say, the Soviet industrialization debate of the 1920's, did not concern investment strategy but rather the choice of systems, ranging from a welfare capitalist to a Libermanesque profits and wages incentive system, and even to a full-fledged market socialism. These were all rejected in favor of comprehensive administrative socialism with heavy reliance on nonmonetary incentives for both managers and workers. The debate was thus decisively settled by 1966 when Cuban socialism embarked more fully on the road mapped for it by Guevara.

18. A list of the textbooks used appears in the Cuban Economic Research Project's *Cuba, Agriculture and Planning* (Coral Gables: University of Miami Press, 1965), p. 5. The key role of the Chilean Marxists is discussed in Claudio Véliz, "The New Cuban Industrial Policy, "*The World Today*, September, 1963.

19. On the debate our best original source is *Cuba Socialista* from 1963 to 1965. For a survey see S. de Santis, "Debate sobre la gestión socialista en Cuba," *Cuadernos de Ruedo Ibérico* (France), 1967 Supplement.

The 26th of July Model

Let us start with the welfare capitalist variant proposed several years before January 1, 1959 and to which Cuba seemed to conform up to about the middle of that year.

The roots of the 26th of July model go as far back as 1953 when Fidel Castro declared that, in addition to a welfare capitalist and anti-latifundist agrarian reform,

> A revolutionary government with the support of the public, after cleaning up the nation's institutions of graft and corruption, will immediately proceed to industrialize the country, mobilizing all of its inactive capital of more than 1.5 billion (pesos) through the National Bank and the Agricultural and Industrial Development Bank. It will submit this task for study, direction, and planning and execution by technicians and men of absolute competence . . .[20]

The planning system outlined by Fidel Castro from 1953 to the first half of 1959, which aimed at implementing the developmental goal of the Cuban Revolution, was described in the first national development blueprint of the Cuban Revolution. This plan document was titled "Economic Thesis of the 26th of July Revolutionary Movement"; its main thesis was:

> Cuba can have an efficient and honest state that will make us all prosperous and whose actions can stimulate, project, finance, combat, or replace private enterprise. That is the thesis of the 26th of July Movement.[21]

The institutional model described in the thesis is similar to what Oskar Lange has elsewhere referred to as the third pattern, combining elements of both capitalistic and socialist

20. From his "La historia me absolverá," in Fidel Castro, *Pensamiento político, económico y social de Fidel Castro* (hereafter referred to as *Pensamiento*) (Havana: Editorial Lex, 1959), p. 44.

21. From "Economic Thesis of the 26th of July Revolutionary Movement, 1957" in *Pensamiento*, p. 92. The Thesis was first published in Mexico City in early 1957.

systems of development.[22] Its general features are briefly the following: It called for central planning measures which worked with the use of markets; political entrepreneurship was to be actively exercised by providing general fiscal, monetary, other monetary-price inducements to private enterprises including direct investment by the government itself. It recommended the creation of a Minister of Economy charged with the drafting of national development plans. Its general planning philosophy was that the "rapid economic development of a country is not generated by the spontaneous workings of economic forces . . . . Cuba ought to eschew the thesis of spontaneity and accept state planning and all of its consequences in order to accelerate its economic development.[23] The document thus contained the blueprint of a national development plan. A yearly growth rate of 7.5 percent was planned and supported strongly by the government sponsorship of a campaign to raise a yearly rate of savings of $200 million. This was a realizable goal since the report mentioned that "the Cuban economy generates an annual rate of savings of more than $200,000,000 with the existing distribution of national income," [24] and there was, according to the report, substantial excess capacity in industry, transport, and other sectors. As excess capacity gradually disappeared, planned savings would rise to $320 million. In ten years' time, the national income growing at a planned 7.5 percent compound rate would double from 1735 billion dollars to $3540 billion, and unemployment of all kinds was expected to disappear by this date, if not sooner.[25] Another important objective of this plan was "to give a growing role to Cuban entrepreneurs and

22. Oskar Lange, *Economic Development, Planning and International Cooperation* (New York: Monthly Review Press, 1963), p. 13.
23. *Pensamiento*, pp. 94–95.
24. Ibid., p. 102.
25. Ibid., p. 104.

the State in the national wealth . . . .[26] For this purpose the State was to use the tool of nationalization or socialization of foreign enterprises. The socialization of large portions of foreign property made the professed nationalism of the leaders believable to the Cuban masses and constituted a sort of founding act. In many cases, such as Indonesia and Ghana, nationalization stopped short of a Marxist-Leninist stage but in Cuba it led to this. For most of 1959, it looked like the new government would simply implement the welfarist and growth aims of the 26th of July model. In that year an official invitation was extended to a group of experts from the United Nations and the Economic Commission for Latin America. This Commission was headed by the Mexican Marxist, Juan Noyola, and it set the groundwork for planning and recommending projects compatible with the planning system envisioned in the 26th of July model. In a similar spirit, the United Nation's experts from the Economic Commission for Latin America (ECLA) and the Food and Agricultural Organization (FAO) worked on projects for inclusion in a more detailed, project-oriented development program, and the first Five Year Agricultural Plan of 1961–1965 was based on work done by Jacques Chonchol of the FAO.[27] As late as February 1960, the incumbent Minister of Finance, Rufo López Fresquet, invited foreign experts such as Kenneth E. Boulding of the University of Michigan and Ingrav Svennilson of the Swedish Planning Committee to give lectures in planning in February, 1960. In lectures to officials they endorsed reforms and planning methods compatible with the 26th of July Model.[28] If it so pleases the reader he can with good arguments view the 26th of July thesis as a mixed allocational and ownership system leaning heavily towards liberal

26. *Pensamiento*, p. 97.

27. Max Nolff in Dudley Seers, ed., *Cuba, the Economic and Social Revolution* (Chapel Hill: University of North Carolina Press, 1964), pp. 326–27; 422, note 3.

28. *Cuba, Agriculture and Planning*, p. 4.

socialism because of its heavy welfarist provisions and strong reliance on state entrepreneurship and planning. This shows very clearly in the provision for the formation of agricultural cooperatives among independent owners actively guided by a strong state agricultural agency. In industry the revolutionary government planned to "grant workers and employees the rights to participate in 30 percent of the profits of all industrial, mercantile, and mining enterprises, including sugar cane mills"; and landless sugar cultivators would participate in 50 percent of the net income from cane.[29] But the liberal socialist reforms of 1959 seemed to have been merely a stage on the road towards the attempt at realizing a classical Marxist state.

From Libermanism to Market Socialism

The lynch-pin of the major controversy on the choice of systems really centered around the desire of the Guevaraists to implement the relative primacy of moral versus material incentives in the management of the firm and the lack of sufficient concern for this goal by the Cuban Libermanists and those who would carry Libermanism beyond its administrative confines into market socialism. At first, the Guevaraists tied themselves, unnecessarily in the writer's view, to the hypothesis that the primacy of moral incentives was compatible with only one kind of centralized management of the firm. The essence of this centralized management was the accounting and financial incorporation of the firm in the state budget. Later, some of them seem to have become more flexible in experimenting with a limited form of *khozraschet* under which the enterprise is made to act more professionally as an independent accounting unit responsible for its "profits and losses." In both forms of centralized management, managerial and administrative staff can theoretically be made to internalize the value of selfless production rather than being primarily

29. *Pensamiento,* pp. 39–40.

motivated by highly variable bonuses tied to either sales or profits (or even gross volume of production). However, the domestic and foreign opponents of the Guevaraist system argued for expanding the concept of *khozraschet* (financial self-sufficiency) to include additional rules resembling Libermanist practice either in the Soviet Union or in capitalist market systems.

A major critic, and one of the earliest, of the Guevaraist mode of enterprise management was Cuba's Marxist consultant from France, René Dumont. He offered his proposals for reform on several known occasions, in May and August of the year 1960, and in September of 1963. In these proposals, Dumont urged the Cuban leaders to adopt various market-oriented measures which, in effect, would have led Cuban society towards a regulated market system based primarily on the use of material incentives. It was for this reason that Guevara rejected these features of his recommendations. Dumont proposed such major reforms as the restoration of the profit and pricing system of the market as the main regulators of both production and consumer goods allocation, especially in the peculiar conditions of agriculture; the formation of producers' cooperatives in that context; the charging of differential rent on state lands and interest and amortization on liquid capital provided by the state. True, he was chiefly interested in agricultural organization, but his proposals spilled over into attacks against centralized materials allocation and management of the firm like a government office in favor of market solvency and accounting. He also urged cooperatives among small artisans, among firms in the distributive field, and among other small industries. In large and heavy industry, he seemed to favor state ownership, but with significantly more decentralization.[30]

30. René Dumont, *Cuba: Socialisme et Développement* (Paris: Editions du Seuil, 1964), p. 141, *et passim*. He makes the same points in his chapter on Cuba in *Lands Alive* (New York: MR Press, 1965). First published in French in 1961.

On the output side, his proposals would free the enterprise, especially in agriculture, from the behaviorial rule of executing central orders with respect to gross physical yields and with respect also to the input-utilization instructions. He would have them replaced by the general rule of having firms make profits and by allowing inter-enterprise trade in intermediate goods thus freeing them from the central allocators and materials balancers. Current decisions and a limited amount of decentralized investment would be left to self-administered enterprises whose myriads of separate plans would be coordinated and steered through the profit-market system. Dumont's principal reason for advocating the profit-market steering of decision units was the widespread coordinative disorder he observed in the field. This organizing function (coordinative planning) absorbed much of the time of planners and a bureaucracy in the worst sense emerged. Dumont was disheartened by these and wrote that coordination of the various units could be turned over to the market. Central planners, in his scheme, would then be freed to perform developmental planning tasks. With regard to this long-range planning, he also favored use of fiscal and monetary measures reminiscent of Yugoslavia. His other reason was the reckless investment decisions and lack of cost discipline and responsibility which he noted. The introduction of profit steering and self-management, he argued, would automatically enforce discipline.[31]

In an effort to show that this model of decentralized market management was consistent with the original provisions of the Agrarian Reform Law of May 1959, he wrote: "Besides, the law for Agrarian reform does provide that the INRA will nominate the administrators of cooperatives, and promises them the best training in the initial stages (*until the law grants them greater autonomy*). If the experiment with autonomy is really with responsibility, which it will be if it involves profitability at the same time, then it is important to

31. Dumont, *Cuba: Socialisme et Développement*, pp. 50, 134, 139–46.

reach this second stage. Upon it depends . . . the whole future of planning. Upon it, above all, depends the democratization of the economy . . . ." [32] The extreme complexity of the agricultural material, the variability of the weather, and of land and crop conditions, demanded greater empiricism and the ability to make quick decisions on the spot. Hence, Dumont went on, profitability was a more suitable indicator of performance than planned physical yields. Secondly, administrative centralization, he warned, would lead to bureaucratism, and the ". . . . self-importance of bureaucrats, leads to inadequacies of abstract management, and then to political nepotism which replaces all the planners by yes-men." [33]

In sum the Dumont proposals offered an alternative form of planning organization which represented in Cuba a new brand of Marxian thought variously referred to as the profit-oriented school, liberal Marxist, or market socialist. Dumont represented the pragmatic socialist approach when, for example, he criticized the early comprehensive nationalization of capital assets including retail trade. During his interview with Ernesto Guevara in mid-August of 1960, in which he wished to discuss the main proposals he had earlier submitted, Dumont learned of Guevara's opposition to them. Guevara talked of his interest in the moral question of building a new man motivated mainly by moral incentives. Dumont wrote: " 'Che' developed then a very interesting position, a kind of idealized vision of socialist man, who has become a stranger to the commercial aspect of things, and who works for society no longer with the motive of personal gain . . . . He did not see in Soviet man a true specimen of a new humanity because he did not find him really different from the Yankee. He [Guevara] would refuse to participate consciously in the creation in Cuba of "a second North American society. . . ." [34]

32. Dumont, *Cuba: Socialisme et Développement*, p. 102.
33. Ibid., p. 101.
34. Ibid., p. 54.

There was an able and articulate group of Cuban planners whose sympathy for Dumont's Libermanist and market-
oriented proposals became public about two years later. They
were in two camps; those who would expand the concept
of *khozraschet* to include Libermanist methods of decentralizing the administrative system and those who would expand
it to include market socialism. The latter often disguised
their market orientation, but both camps were united in their
relative lack of concern for ensuring the primacy of moral
incentives. Specifically, they centered their attack on the
budgetary system of management of the firm and argued for
the introduction of *khozraschet*. They partially succeeded
in their attack in inducing the central policymakers to intro-
duce the latter method of financial management in a significant
number of enterprises; but they failed in the sense that the
khozraschet practiced in Cuba did not go as far as they
wished. Since 1966 and in Cuban enterprises today, the sub-
ordination of enterprises to a central authority has been reasserted and accounting transactions among enterprises and
with the central authority de-emphasized. Managers presumably work on the basis of nonmonetary or moral incentives
in the manner of government employees who render services
to the public independently of the changing pattern of monetary returns.

It soon became apparent in the course of the debate that
the profit-oriented decentralists did not confine their proposals
to a limited form of *khozraschet* acceptable to the Guevaraists. Their horizon included other forms of decentralization.
Let us explain this further although a clearer and more
thorough explanation of the concepts which follow will be
postponed until the next chapter. "Self-finance" was known
under two Spanish names in Cuba—a source of some confusion in the debate, as we shall see. It was known under either
sistema autofinanciero or *autonomía económica*. Its main
organizational rules were: the enterprise should keep its own
set of accounts, cover its cost, and only after calculating its

net income for the accounting period should it make all fixed contributions to the state budget. *Autonomía económica* or "self-finance" was, however, defined to include additional characteristics which were objectionable to the administrative centralists. This radicalized form of *khozraschet* included such provisions as the empowering of enterprises to transact among themselves on the basis of direct relations based on commercial trade (*compraventa*). The profit-oriented decentralists stressed the need to have the enterprise not only make use of short-term bank credits in accordance with the more conservative version of *khozraschet*, but also to make amounts of decentralized investment from an enterprise fund and the sale of idle equipment.[35] Thus the supporters of "self-finance" threatened the existence of central allocation of intermediate goods—the hallmark of the centrally administered Guevaraist system.[36]

Guevara saw through the hesitant market-orientation of the supporters of private material incentives. He warned against using the pre-1966 Soviet *khozraschet* interchangeably with the Cuban term, *autonomía económica*.[37] The latter, he argued, was being used by its supporters as a cover for introducing the Libermanist mode of decentralization and hid an orientation in favor of market-like behavior. Thus, in 1963 and 1964, Guevara's Ministry of Industries through its journal, *Nuestra Industria* joined the world-wide socialist controversy on material versus moral incentives that ensued after Liberman's September, 1962 article in *Pravda*. It argued strongly against the cardinal principle of Libermanism—decentraliza-

35. Joaquín Infante. "Características del funcionamiento de la empresa autofinanciada," *Cuba Socialista*, June, 1964, pp. 34, 43–44.

36. On Guevara's articles on these matters see *Venceremos, The Speeches and Writings of Che Guevara*, J. Gerassi, ed. (New York: Macmillan, 1968). On the decentralist position the best sources are the 1963–1965 issues of *Cuba Socialista* and *Nuestra Industria: Revista Económica*.

37. Guevara's article in *Cuba Socialista*, March 1965, pp. 32–33.

tion of the administrative system on the basis of private material incentives tied to either sales or profitability.

The radical humanists and revolutionary intellectuals who led the Cuban revolution typified a dislike for market institutions and consequently admired the administrative solution to the resource allocation problem. James O'Connor noted this same bias and defends it. "The revolutionary leadership had from the outset a strong bias in the direction of industrial consolidation and central physical planning . . . ." for the reason that "the organization of industry and market structures in pre-revolutionary Cuba contributed to the island's stagnation, and from the standpoint of sheer economic rationality, the nationalization, consolidation, and planning of industry could only work to the ultimate advantage of Cuban economic development." [38] This dogma carries a great deal of prestige. A manifesto by more than sixty of Latin America's leading intellectuals shows this preference for a nonmarket "big push":

> In order to make planning effective, it is essential that it decisively influence the rate and structure of investment itself and not just the public sector in the field of infrastructure: . . . that the fundamental economic decisions arise from the plan and not be based on the market mechanism nor should they be based on objectives different from that of planning the accelerated and independent development of our countries . . .[39]

Indeed, the quotation above is a paraphrase of the big-push and balanced growth theories of early modern development theory.[40]

38. James O'Connor, "Industrial Organization in the Old and New Cubas," *Science and Society*, Spring, 1966, pp. 176, 189.

39. "The Declaration of Latin American Economists," *Desarrollo* (Bogotá, Colombia, January 1, 1966), pp. 7–8.

40. Maurice Dobb, *Economic Growth and Planning* (New York: Monthly Review Press, 1960), Chapter 1; Paul A. Baran, "On the Political Economy of Backwardness," reprinted in A. N. Agarwala

An Alternative Hypothesis

If rapid modernization and social welfare were the only main goals of the radical intellectuals who headed the Cuban revolution, the choice of organizational means for implementing those goals is indeterminate. They could have been achieved by any of the rejected alternative systems discussed earlier since any of these are compatible with a high rate of investment and redistribution of the national product in favor of the lower income classes. Cubanization of the largest means of production could theoretically have been achieved in any of the rejected systems. In view of these remarks, the determining element in the choice among several systems seems to have been ideological and owed much to classical (anti-market egalitarian) Marxism. The other face of this ideological position is the preference for the administrative solution to the resource allocation problem. This natural inclination to arrange resources by resort to a rational bureaucratic (administrative) set-up was particularly popular among Latin American radical intellectuals at the time. The reason is due to its prestige in intellectual circles abroad under the name of "non-market big-push." The thesis here being proposed is that the main leaders possessed an ideology prior to their assumption of power and soon went about constructing an egalitarian variant of administrative socialism. The pace of organizational destruction and reconstruction was rapid so that by late 1959 or early 1960 the market capitalist system had been effectively eliminated. This does not mean that a smoothly functioning administration replaced the market immediately. In fact, there was little coordinated central planning during the early period of state ownership of the means of production. A kind of

and S. P. Singh (eds.,) *The Economics of Underdevelopment* (New York: Oxford University Press, 1963); also in the latter, see the articles by Nurkse, Rosenstein-Rodan, and Scitovsky.

administrative socialist laissez-faire called by the Cubans *por la libre* (free-wheeling) reigned from late 1959 through 1962 and possibly up to early 1963. Boorstein's eyewitness account of this transitional period from a welfare market capitalism to administrative socialism is endearing for its candor and instructive for its stress on the immense complexity of devising administrative counterparts to the coordinative jobs performed by markets;[41] here his authoritative description is worth recalling briefly. *Por la libre*, which literally means unrestrained activity, seems to have become serious in late 1959 when the drive to paralyze the market system by freezing prices and issuing a plethora of quantity controls was accelerated and had succeeded in abolishing the market. The rebel army officers who mainly replaced fleeing *técnicos* and managers were set free to use their judgment—often arbitrary—in determining their output mix and production technologies. They scrounged for inputs wherever ingenuity, drive and other means led them, usually at the doors of harassed and acquiescent monetary and foreign-exchange officials (of which Boorstein was one). The latter tried to exercise parsimony but often relented in granting liberal credits. The resulting disorganization or "unsystem"—which was neither market nor a coordinated administrative system—was characterized by inflation, depletion of foreign-exchange, spoilage from uncoordinated storage facilities and deliveries, quality deterioration, arbitrary investment-making and so on. The challenge-and-response ("blow-counterblow") theory about the origins of socialism in Cuba seems to apply more to the logic of how—having abolished the price-profit-or-perish commands of the market which instructed and disciplined managers in their activities—the surprised planners were

41. Edward Boorstein, *The Economic Transformation of Cuba* (New York: Monthly Review, 1968). There are a few similarities here to Chilean socialism, whose transformation into either the administrative or market variant is not yet clear.

hard pressed to devise administrative counterparts to the co-ordinative jobs of markets they had abolished in an escalating pattern. Boorstein regards 1963 as a milestone although Guevara [42] would have cited a date a year later. With flexibility and prodigious effort, a workable central administration had finally been installed.

42. Speaking in May, 1963, Guevara predicted: "After this year, we will be able to say truthfully that the administrative apparatus actually directs the industry of the country." *May Day Speech to Labor-1963* (New York: Fair Play for Cuba Committee, 1963), p. 14.

CHAPTER TWO

Moral Incentives
as a Non-Libermanist Mode of
Managerial Behavior

Moral Incentives and Decentralization

In the preceding chapter it was suggested that the early major
controversy in Cuba revolved around the choice of a system
that would foster a desirable mix between moral and material
incentives. The anti-Guevaraists, in the ultimate analysis, did
not value moral incentives as much as the Guevaraists, and
it was the latter's values that eventually and decisively triumphed by late 1966. To a large extent this description of the
entire resource-allocating device of moral incentives applies
to China particularly during the "Great Leap Forward" era
of 1958–1961, and the current period after the Cultural Revolution initiated in late 1965 and early 1966. Like China in the
early years of the Communist assumption of power, Cuba,
too, borrowed heavily from the then existing Soviet-type
model; later both countries departed from it in a significant
way. The similarities between China and Cuba are so striking
that one is tempted to suggest the same passionate copying of
an alternative Communist model—the Chinese model after
1957 this time. There is a grain of truth here since in China,
the mechanism of moral incentives, or what Vogel calls by

the name "voluntarism," preceded its use in Cuba.[1] But there is more truth, it seems, in saying that the Maoists and Guevaraists arrived at similar systemic solutions by independent discovery. Both groups were eager to actualize the classical socialist anti-market and egalitarian values; both were professedly anti-bureaucratic.

Vogel's description of moral incentives in China seems to be the most systematic one we have of it as a form of social organization. He describes it as an essentially decentralist compliance system by which the leadership minimizes dissatisfaction among the citizenry while making them do what otherwise they would not wish to do. What makes the mechanism decentralist or voluntary is the use of persuasion, promises, and the ingenious manipulation of a rich array of symbolic awards in exchange for compliance.[2] Sanctions are used too, as part of that mechanism, such as the myriad difficulties of all kinds that the non-volunteer may encounter in the future; but what makes them consistent with a decentralist mechanism is their indirect nature. Punishments (corresponding to the hunger of the market incentive system) are deliberately vague and may not even be meted out in many cases.

In this study, the subject is approached in detail as a resource-allocating device alternative to the market principle of organization and doctrinally founded on some version of "from each his ability, to each his need." Moreover, the subject is also approached as a non-Libermanist technique of decentralizing and de-bureaucratizing the centrally administrative system. By a Libermanist productive system, let us recall, is meant one where the firm seeks maximum monetary returns

1. Ezra F. Vogel, "Voluntarism and Social Control," in Donald W. Treadgold, ed., *Soviet and Chinese Communism* (Seattle: University of Washington Press, 1967), pp. 168–84.

2. G. William Skinner and Edwin A. Winckler's treatment of the subject is similar. See their "Compliance Succession in Rural Communist China: A Cyclical Theory," in A. Etzioni, ed., *Complex Organizations, A Sociological Reader*, 2nd ed. (New York: Holt, Rinehart and Winston, 1969).

by offering private material and monetary incentives in the process. The other works on moral incentives in China and Cuba deal with it mainly as a complementary device to material incentives for increasing work incentives in given places; here it is also dealt with as a substitute allocational device for the market—and as a non-Libermanist mode of enterprise management.

One of the major aims cf the revolutionary offensive in late 1966 to the present was the construction of communism in its organizational-allocative sense. Aside from eventually raising the rate of investment to a dramatic, nearly one-third of national income, the other major aim was to institutionalize the mechanism of moral incentives as deeply as possible by teaching all Cubans the rightness and necessity of working more for community benefits than for one's private interest. This is what the main policymakers understood by *estímulo moral* or *conciencia comunista* and by the concept of creating the new man. But they regarded *conciencia* also as a technique of partially decentralizing the administrative planning apparatus since, ideally, it is a nonmarket device whereby managers and workers could be trusted to fulfill centrally defined community goals with a minimum of supervision. *Conciencia* meant that managers, including workers, intensify their efforts in production and choose socially needed tasks in exchange for socially approved symbols of praise and merit—not money. To inculcate this new work ethic, a cultural revolution was unleashed again or, at least, intensified to a dramatically higher pitch in late 1966. As in China, the many organizations that emerged after the revolution, at least one of which every Cuban belonged to, became the main vehicles for institutionalizing the mechanism of *estímulo moral* on a nation-wide basis. Not least of this was the Communist Party, which could be entrusted with the work of exerting pressure and seeing to it that community goals took precedence in the activities of managers and workers.

In the previous chapter, we noted the early preference

for the primacy of moral incentives shown by Cuba's most powerful planner at this time—Dr. Ernesto "Che" Guevara. In the great debate, he and his well-placed followers argued for the primacy of moral incentives in the sphere of managerial behavior, not just in the organization of labor. In the sphere of managerial behavior, they contended that moral incentives could be implemented best in a type of central planning where the firm acted like a government office with staff whose salaries did not vary with the services they rendered to the public. This would be behavior compatible with the ethic of "from each according to his ability." Thus the Guevaraists preferred and retained the prevailing form of enterprise management and financing reminiscent of Soviet War Communism in which firms were financially incorporated into the state budget, from which all expenditures came and to which all revenues flowed directly. This was the practice we called budget finance in the previous chapter. In contrast to this, the main method used in China and the Soviet Union is known as self-finance or *khozraschet*. It is also the method used in capitalist market societies, for its essence is that firms be independent accounting units responsible for their own financial survival. Experiments in self-finance were tried in Cuba and there was an attempt, supported by the anti-Guevaraists, to widen its application to a larger number of enterprises. It will now be shown, however, that the two divergent modes of financing the Cuban firm are different merely on a superficial level. They are the same in essence, and that essence is defined by the fact that all state enterprises are run like government offices from state financial allocations independently of their revenues.

The Cuban firm is non-Libermanist since a Libermanist firm is chiefly concerned with making a profit or enhancing sales or a combination of both, and in the process offers private material incentives in the form of graduated salaries and bonuses tied to the main monetary objectives. Thus, in a Libermanist system, the principal allocative-incentive mechanism for managers and workers alike is the labor market; and total real income bears a relation to the manager's and worker's contribution to profits or sales. The Soviet Union of the post-1966 period—as well as Yugoslavia, Hungary, and others in Eastern Europe at the present time—are Libermanist in the sense defined in the preceding remarks. But most of the members of that kind of productive organization are capitalist market societies. Aside from an alternative cultural morality in the latter type of countries which regards profit-making ethically neutral, if not desirable, the main social function of Libermanism is to decentralize the allocation of resources to their various competing uses. In the Eastern European context, decentralization through the practice of Libermanism takes place within an administrative allocational system—by tying managerial and labor performance to profitability or a combined index of profitability and sales. In the moral culture being created in Cuba and China the idea of maximizing monetary returns and offering private monetary incentives in the process is regarded as immoral and goes by the name of "revisionism" and "economism". True, managers in both countries are constantly reminded to do careful accounting of costs and not to disregard profits entirely, but these concepts designate different managerial practices than are found in Libermanist countries. The main goal of the Cuban and Chinese firm is maximum physical output as laid down by planning bodies, not profits or sales; and the main inputs are centrally allocated. Moreover, costs exclude charges for the use of capital and prices are far more removed from their scarcity values than in Libermanist countries. And in Cuba and China alike, there are no material incentive funds out of profits or sales such as exist in Libermanist Eastern Europe. Monetary and material incentives, largely in the form of differentiated time payments, exist in both countries, of course. This only means, however, that the mechanism of moral incentives operates imperfectly. In the appendix * it is

* Pages 141–56.

argued that some mixture of moral and material incentives are compatible even in a market society, but the overwhelming weight of material stimulation in such a mixture does not satisfy the combination desired by a committed socialist who is anxious to see moral incentives dominate the whole society. We may view the mechanism of moral incentives as an organizational building block based on feelings of community solidarity; the market on the other hand rests chiefly on production for the sake of self-determined goals—often of a mainly monetary and material nature. It is for these reasons that the classical socialists in Cuba and China—and elsewhere—hold the relationship between moral incentives and market-material stimulation as one of basic incompatibility.

This study proposes, then, that a necessary condition for finding out whether a society relies *primarily* on moral incentives is to see whether it has succeeded in abolishing the labor market as the chief allocating and motivating device. It shall be shown here that Cuba passes this test—and China, too, to a lesser extent. This test is, of course, not sufficient; but it is one justified by the historical context of the debate in the socialist world on the relative primacy between moral and material incentives.

The previous discussion suggests that a highly unequal system of private material incentives can be tied to any success indicator. Before the Soviet Union entered its Liberman-ist phase, the chief criterion on which bonuses depended was fulfillment and overfulfillment of physical production. The income differentials this produced often surpassed those in many capitalist countries—with the exception of the few on top of the capitalist income distribution. In Cuba and China, there are no bonuses for directors, vice-directors and party secretaries.[3] Moreover, the modest salary ranges are nullified or made more egalitarian by a great deal of consumer ration-

3. Barry Richman, "Capitalists and Managers in Communist China," *Harvard Business Review*, Jan.–Feb., 1967, p. 65. Other

ing, subsidized consumption and free social services in both countries. And material incentives for middle to lower personnel are being de-emphasized in favor of moral incentives.

Note that the mechanism of moral incentives is compatible with the practice of *khozrascbet*, as Chinese experience bears out. It is also theoretically possible with firm production for an intermediate and consumer goods market. What charges the air of the ideological debate on moral versus material incentives is that the idea of production for monetary returns is abhorrent as well to the classical Marxists who set policy in Cuba and China—since it is the chief aim of the capitalist firm. But this position does not seem strictly implied by the adherence to the primary role of moral incentives which requires that only the labor market be abolished.

Self-finance or *khozraschet* has various degrees of development, ranging from its conservative forms in Cuba and China to its Libermanist stage in the Soviet Union, and to its climactic radicalization in Yugoslav market socialism. In the Soviet Union, even before its Libermanist phase, self-finance was for a long time associated with imperfect labor markets and private material incentives that often produced income disparities among workers greater than in many capitalist countries. The Guevaraists and Maoists did not think of self-finance in those terms. It would seem that to make the firm's residual goal of profit-making meaningful in the system of self-finance, the director's and worker's salary may have to be partially tied to that secondary success indicator. And the greater role of money in this system (as partial command over goods and people) would give managers greater power to use it for their purposes, which may not always coincide

sources on the Chinese firm are articles on the subject in the February, 1970 issue of the theoretical journal, *Red Flag;* V. King, "Industrial Enterprise Planning Process in China," *The China Mainland Review,* March, 1967; Franz Schurmann, *Ideology and Organization in Communist China* (University of California Press, 1966).

with centralized community values. It is perhaps in these senses that Guevara viewed the supporters of self-finance with suspicion and opposed them—particularly when the latter began using another Cuban term *autonomía económica* for *autofinanciamiento* (self-finance). The Cuban supporters of self-finance seem to have had the more liberal Soviet form in mind—one associated with the primacy of material incentives. Guevara argued that this would lead to the splitting of working class solidarity into various competing income groups, and enhance group individualism in the firm as well as competition for private material gains.

It is in the light of the preceding remarks that we should view the organization of the Cuban firm and the heavy attack to which it was subjected in the first half of the 1960's by a notable group of Cuban planners and foreign consultants in Cuba. James O'Connor's view that this debate was a minor technical disagreement among the planners concerning methods of accounting is superficial.[4] And so too are the usual accounts of this controversy which emphasize disagreements among the policymakers in regard to allowing or not allowing the firm to borrow short-term credit from the state bank; or whether or not rental charges on capital should be made; and whether or not socialist firms produce 'traded commodities' or merely 'transferred products.'[5] The debate embraced all these questions and other additional points, but it went much deeper and centered around the key issue of choosing a managerial system that could best implement heavier reliance on moral versus material incentives. Thus the debate concerned the choice of systems itself.

4. James O'Connor, his letter in *Commentary*, May, 1964.
5. For example, S. de Santis, "Debate sobre la gestión socialista en Cuba," *Cuadernos de Ruedo Ibérico* (France), 1967 Supplement.

Organization of the Firm [6]

The unit of production—the firm—in Cuba are the huge trusts called *consolidado* and *combinado*, respectively. The former is a consolidated enterprise made up of industrial factories and shops of the pre-socialist period, merged under a common management on the basis of the horizontal criterion of sameness of products. The number of factories in each varied from a few to several hundred establishments—for example, the Flour Consolidated Enterprise comprised 800 in the mid-1960's. But on the average, the consolidated enterprise administered 10 to 15 factories.[7]

As a direct result of Premier Castro's criticism of the inefficiency of the *consolidado*, a new trust, the *combinado*, appeared near the mid-1960's, grouping factories vertically under one management. Thus *Cubatabaco*, the tobacco combine, merged all the manufacturing stages of that product together including its domestic and foreign distribution. Since virtually all nonagricultural property is in state hands, consolidated enterprise and combines are the typical units in that major sector. In agriculture, the *agrupación* corresponds to the *consolidado* in industry. These managerial units came into being in the second semester of 1963 as a result of the Second Agrarian Reform. Before that reform, state farms were excess-

6. I deal with the structure and planning of the Cuban firm in detail in my article "Managing and Financing the Cuban Firm like a Government Office," in C. Mesa-Lago, ed., *Revolutionary Change in Cuba: Polity, Economy, Society* (Pittsburgh: The University of Pittsburgh Press, 1971).

7. Juan M. Castiñeiras, "La industria ligera en la etapa actual," *Cuba Socialista*, June, 1964, pp. 4–5; also JUCEPLAN. "El desarrollo industrial de Cuba," *Cuba Socialista*, May, 1966, p. 103. See also, "Reglamento orgánico de las empresas consolidadas del Ministerio de Industrias," *Gaceta Oficial*, August 9, 1961. Additional documentation is cited in my cited article.

ively centralized under the general administration for state farms headquartered in Havana. The *agrupación* is made up of several state farms in the same region. Although a state farm forms an administrative unit, it is under the managerial supervision of the *agrupación* in regard to key financial, technological, and administrative matters.[8] Like the *consolidado* and *combinado,* each *agrupación* has a director assisted by an administrative council. The state farms administered by it have a similar organizational chart except that each state farm is made up of lots of varying sizes with a permanent brigade of workers permanently attached to them.

The Cuban state farm is like the Soviet *sovkhoz.* Workers receive fixed wages, subsidized housing, free medical services, and social security. Until 1967 they were allowed a small vegetable garden, but even then, selling produce from it and raising livestock on it were "illegal." The state farm embraced 70 percent of the land area available for cultivation; the remainder is nominally owned by small farmers. I say nominally since the rules governing their use have effectively converted most of them into some hybrid kind of state property. They are integrated into the Small Farmers Association (ANAP) under the control of the Ministry of Agriculture's (INRA's) Vice-Ministry of Private Production. After the mid-1960's their inputs have increasingly been supplied by the state which in return has demanded most of the "private" sector's output at prices fixed by the state.

In addition to state farms, there are state firms in agriculture similar to the Machine Tractor Stations of Soviet experience; it services the "private" sector as well. Cooperatives of the Soviet variety (*kolkhoz*) sharply declined in mid-1962 and are negligible today.

Estimates of the number of *agrupaciones* by the mid-1960's ranged from 56 to 80 while state farm estimates varied

8. Carlos Rafael Rodríguez, "El nuevo camino de la agricultura cubana," *Cuba Socialista,* November, 1963, p. 83.

from 577 to 800.[9] At roughly the time of the introduction of the industrial combine, a significant experiment initiated in agriculture was the agricultural combine—significant since it rarely applies in other Communist countries. The agricultural combines are really agro-industrial trusts that vertically join under one management the planting and harvesting stages to the higher manufacturing phases that the particular product undergoes, and finally to its domestic distribution and export. The agricultural combine, like its counterpart in industry, functions like a central ministry and is regarded also as a superior planning body. At the present time, however, little is known about its operations.[10] This is partly due to the lack of information that has become more serious since late 1966. We know, however, the general behavioral principles which govern the activity of the Cuban firm, and these will be described below.

Budgetary Finance

The main method of financing the Cuban firm is the system of state budgetary financing of the firm. It started in industry and was the method used in all state enterprises from 1961 to 1963. At around the start of 1964 elements of what we referred to as self-finance were introduced in agriculture at the level of the *agrupación* and in foreign trade but do not seem to have matured. In practice, self-finance turned out to be an indirect form or an impure kind of state budgetary financing. Since 1965, there has been a progressive tendency towards more direct forms of budgetary financing.

The financial and managerial system called budgetary or

9. G. L. Beckford, "A Note on Agricultural Organization and Planning in Cuba," *Caribbean Studies*, October, 1966; Michel Gutelman, *L'agriculture socialisée à Cuba* (Paris, 1967).

10. René Dumont merely mentions the combine in his *Cuba: est-il socialiste?* (Paris, 1970), p. 72.

budget finance operated in the following manner. All the
state firms' accounts were simply lumped together under one
"centralized fund" administered through the National Bank.
Enterprises made direct deposits of their revenues to this account from which they received allocations as well for their
costs of production. Sometime in late 1960 or early 1961, the
"centralized fund" was officially included in the "general
state budget" under the control of the Ministry of Finance in
accounts still held in the National Bank. This tended to shift
power over the nation's financial and credit plans from the
National Bank and from INRA, which at this time had very
enormous financial powers. As a mode of centralized management, however, budget finance stood for a tighter kind of
centralized administrative management of the firm than the
then current Soviet practice of *khozraschet*. In both modes
of centralized management, the firm's primary goal is the
maximization of physical output but budget finance included
these other behavioral or organizational rules.

a) Firms receive allocations of funds for their expenses over a
   definite period, say a trimester, *before* producing its income . . .
b) moral incentives are the principal method of stimulating and
   improving production with material incentives as a com-
   plement.
c) firms are subject to "control by cost [indices]"
d) in being linked to the state budget for all of its costs and
   revenues, firms never make use of bank credit in a direct
   way.[11]

The rationale for this system is contained in this statement
by the Minister of Finance at that time—Luis Alvarez Rom:

The receipts and payments among enterprises, in our view, are
nothing more than compensating acts in which the monetary

11. Marcelo Fernández Font, "Desarrollo y funciones de la banca
socialista en Cuba," *Cuba Socialista*, February, 1964, p. 45.

expression shown by the use of a bank document is purely of an arithmetic or accounting nature. It is the instrument used by the bank in its role as the center of social accounting to register the flow of the receipt and delivery of products. In having no bank accounts of its own, the enterprise automatically delivers all of its revenues to the national budget, thus eliminating the necessity of the state having to charge its share of the enterprise profits. . . .[12]

Endorsing the same passage, Guevara added:

"Since the enterprise does not retain nor accumulate funds of its own . . . . it is unnecessary to tax or to lend at interest." [13]

The enterprise takes initiative in preparing its financial and credit plan within rules laid down by the Central Planning Board, the Finance Ministry, and the ministry or central organization to which the firm belongs. Its financial plan is summarized in three accounts: an income account, an expense account, and a budget account listing its financial relations with the state budget.[14] These financial plans are of course reviewed and modified by a superior planning body— the ministry and central organization like INRA—which submits it to the Finance Ministry and the National bank at the stipulated date.

The firms' financial allocations are given every trimester or so; they cannot change their financial relations with the state budget without the consent of the Central Planning Board. As mentioned earlier these accounts are handled by branches of the National Bank. Thus "budget units" as well

12. Luis Alvarez Rom, "Sobre el método de análisis de los sistemas de financiamiento," *Cuba Socialista*, July, 1964, p. 77.

13. Ernesto Che Guervara, "La banca, el crédito y el socialismo," *Cuba Socialista*, March, 1964, p. 37.

14. For specimens of the enterprise's financial allocations and accounts, see the documents assembled by the Cuban Research Project, *A Study On Cuba* (Coral Gables, Florida: University of Miami Press, 1964).

as *"khozraschet* units" kept accounts although the latter hand over to or receive from the budget their net revenue or net loss. A Law 1007 passed by the Council of Ministers in early 1962 [15] obliged firms to carry out their payments to each other by means of debits to the purchasers and credits to the supplier's accounts in the National Bank. Commercial credit transactions among them was prohibited. The purpose of the Bank's active role is to make sure funds in the firm's accounts are used for the purposes specified in their production plans; the Bank, too, required the firm to observe the limit of from about 5 to 25 days for collecting payment from customers. The main responsibility for finalizing financial transactions was put on suppliers.[16] Since all the firms kept some form of accounts, were so supervised by the Bank, and were instructed to keep their costs down, it does not seem clear how budget-finance differs markedly from self-finance. Often the contending schools distinguished the two forms of centralized management superficially according to whether the Finance Ministry or the National Bank granted credits to the firm.

Self-Finance

Under self-finance, the firm's primary goal is still fulfillment of the plan, but in addition it

. . . requires socialist enterprises to cover their [current] costs with their own revenues and insure the profitability of production. The state supplies the financing for centralized investments. However, in producing its income part of it is earmarked for decentralized investments proposed by the enterprise and approved by the central planning bodies. This method, which also presupposes the use of bank credits to finance working capital [due to unforeseen factors] permits

15. *Gaceta Oficial*, February 19, 1962, p. 1961.
16. *Gaceta Oficial*, Resolution 3802 of August 16, 1963.

the establishment of an additional control of the economic activities of the enterprises by means of supervision by the banks
[control by the peso].[17]

The description above requires explanation since the essential difference between the two organizational devices is still
somewhat obscure. First of all *autofinanciamiento*, it is implied,
is compatible with the principle of centralized administrative
management. Its use is made pressing by the problem of
incomplete allocational information available to the center;
autofinanciamiento empowers ultimate deciders to determine
the ultimate specifications of their output and input orders
from the center. Thanks to the partial use of money in the
production sector—its chief uses are for aggregation to facilitate communication and evaluation of production—ultimate
deciders possess some command power over resources and
hence are able to sub-specify their instructions from any
number of ultimate products and ultimate technologies so
long as they are guided in this by profitability. In practice,
product and input plans leave little room for choice. With
given product goals, profit maximization reduces to cost
minimization, and since input-utilization plans severely limit
the scope for input substitution, the latter rule approximates
the technical (physical) rule of obtaining the largest output
from each input taken singly.[18] Another feature of self-finance
may be mentioned at this point—"direct relations in the exchange of products among enterprises . . ."[19] This, too, is a
rule to allow deciders to actualize choices for the purpose
defining the ultimate specifications of products they require
from suppliers. But these inter-enterprise contacts take place
within the limits of enterprise supply and delivery plans. It

17. C. Rafael Rodríguez, "El nuevo camino . . . ," p. 88.
18. This argument is found in Gregory Grossman, "Notes Towards a Theory of the Command Economy," reprinted in M. Born-
stein, *Comparative Economic Systems* (Chicago: R. D. Irwin, 1965).
19. M. Fernández Font, "Desarrollo . . ." p. 44.

need not lead as Guevara feared to "mercantile buying and selling in the state sector." [20] But in regard to the leading role of material incentives, Guevara seems to be right in thinking that the system of self-finance would enhance group individualism biased towards the search for material gains.[21] This was admitted by his critics but justified as historical necessity. The reasons seem obvious. Any decentralization which bolsters the power of ultimate deciders to actualize their choices is likely to foster hedonic profit-making unless dampened by unusually strong cultural factors. Also, to make the firm's residual goal of profit-making meaningful, the director's and worker's salaries may need to be tied to that success indicator either in the form of a director's fund for amenities or individual bonuses.

Reversing the Trend to Maximize the Budget

The decision to experiment with self-finance was made as a result of unintended results induced in 1960–1963 and which were partially blamed on the system of budget-finance. During this period socialist administrators of industrial and agricultural enterprises behaved as if their main objective was to maximize their budgets. Although they were committed to the maximizing of physical output they tried to do so by neglecting costs and even by neglecting to collect payment from their customers as required by Law 1007. Thus deficits mounted and administrators were constrained to request increases in their budget allocations. Basing himself on the National Bank's registry, the Bank president complained in early 1964 that "some of these enterprises do not appear motivated in collecting payment for their merchandise and services because their costs are covered and for them it only means not depositing revenues to the [state] budget." The

20. Guevara, "La Banca . . .", p. 36.
21. Ibid., p. 37 et passim.

rules obliging firms to pay and collect promptly (Law 1007) "was violated thousands of times with a value of millions of pesos weekly, an average of 20,000 weekly violations with a value of 20 million pesos." [22]

The financial disorganization among firms resulted in a directive of the Revolutionary Government in mid-1963 to restore "financial order in the enterprises, the reduction of costs of production, and the raising of labor productivity . . ." [23] Part of the solution was the initiation of the first rules of *autofinanciamiento* around the start of the year 1964 in agricultural and foreign trade enterprises. [24] These initial rules pertained to the grant of power to firms to make use of bank credits on terms set by the bank regarding their use, its amortization schedule and material guarantees for the loan such as raw materials, goods-in-process, fuel, and the like. Another rule enjoined enterprises to be solvent.

Budget Finance without the Finance Ministry

To some extent the debate over budget—versus self-finance was a power competition among key persons in the central planning bodies for control over national financial planning. This seems clear from the descriptions of the two forms given by the protagonists which give undue emphasis to the relative primacy of the Finance Ministry or the National Bank in granting credits to enterprises and receiving revenues from them. As we saw in both forms firms keep accounts which are supervised by the Bank and in both forms the injunction to reduce costs is given primary importance. Whether the central financial agency is the Finance Ministry or the Bank, or even the powerful INRA, or a committee formed from them seems beside the point. Indeed the Finance

22. M. Fernández Font, "Desarrollo . . .", pp. 45–46.
23. I. Talavera in *Cuba Socialista*, December, 1963, p. 23.
24. M. Fernández Font, "Desarrollo . . .", p. 39.

Ministry was abolished in early 1966 in favor of the Bank. This act by no means signals the eventual demise of the system of budget-finance as a method of enterprise management so long as the firm is managed in a *purely* administrative and highly centralized manner in the style of a government office described, for example, in Lenin's *State and Revolution*. The supporters of budget finance imply that the firm's allocational functions can be very nearly completely specified and structured with responsibility thereby delegated and evaluated in the style of a Weberian rational bureaucracy. This view assumes the accessibility of central planners to sufficient allocational information and its efficient transmission down the administrative hierarchy. According to this persuasion salaried managers and workers, like government employees, can be motivated to supply greater effort and drive by moral prizes of varying social valuations (ranks). Material incentives still have a vital and large role to play in the over-all incentive system but they were to be of secondary importance and limited in scope by a narrow set of wage differences without the use of managerial profit-sharing.[25] The decentralists who supported either a conservative or radical form of *khozraschet* deny these premises of the moral stimulators and supporters of budget finance. The latter picture the allocational problem differently and stress its extreme complexity which makes a great deal of decentralization necessary. Like a ship out in the ocean, the modern enterprise is embedded, too, in this view, in a turbulent and ever constantly changing allocational field of consumer tastes and technological processes. Central managers with the latest computers may not respond quickly enough and the ability of the communications media to trans-

25. To quote Guevara in late 1962, ". . . we always give first place to the educational role, to deepening consciousness, to the call to duty . . . . In addition . . . there are material incentives . . . ." In Adolfo Gilly, *Inside the Cuban Revolution* (New York: Monthly Review Press, 1964) pp. 84–85.

mit enormous loads of information and orders may be limited. As incomes rise and the productive structure grows complex there may be no substitutes to the establishment of direct links among firms guided by material incentives and possibly by the market. In this way firms would be encouraged to meet consumer demand at least cost—demand-prices and cost-prices facilitating the comparison of output with input.

The Guevaraists have questioned the applicability of this analogy to Cuba citing the lesser number of enterprises in Cuba than in the greater Moscow area. They seemingly convincingly argue that, particularly in a small country, firms can be centrally managed at some workable and acceptable level of physical (technical) efficiency like a government bureau.[26] They were extremely concerned with the pervasive problem of production inefficiency but advocated an administrative solution of "making the administrative task of control and supervision even simpler . . . ." One method of achieving this simplification was by instilling moral incentives so as to render much centralized supervision unnecessary. The other method was by means of a comprehensive input-output table and linear programming for certain sectors. By use of the latter method, planners would obtain imputed scarcity prices of inputs from a pre-determined final output plan. Guevara pinned a rather unrealistic amount of hope on such mathematical planning methods and sponsored such studies in the then existing monolithic Ministry of Industries which he headed.[27] There are reasons for deep skepticism in regard to the latter method of simplifying the planning of the firm. The scarcity values in question required for the optimal allocation of inputs to their various competing uses

26. On levels of efficiency and ways of improving the administrative system, see Benjamin Ward, *The Socialist Economy* (New York: Random House, 1967).

27. Guevara, "Consideraciones sobre los costos de producción . . . ," *Nuestra Industria: Revista Económica*, No. 1, 1963.

require the prior existence of a consumer goods market whose scarcity prices are imputed downward to the various inputs. Consumer prices can be derived without the aid of actual markets with the aid of the utility and production curves illustrated in the Appendix, but that method is a mere logical possibility without actual system-wide applications.

Aside from the high costs of computers and information processing and the extremely oversimplified mathematical assumptions required to use the current mathematical planning methods, there are other grounds for doubt. In reality the complexity of a constantly changing technology on the supply side, and tastes on the demand side, may soon make a comprehensive oversimplified mathematical program out of date. And the ability of the mass media to transmit so much information is problematical. There may be no alternative but to decentralize the still highly centralized nature of Cuban planning by establishing direct market links among enterprises on the basis of a more primary role for material incentives, unless of course, *conciencia* proves reasonably effective. A few more years, it seems, are required to assess the workability of moral incentives in general and of the office-like management of the firm in particular. The latter, as well as the former) is being improved, lately with the help of technical input-output programs, yet one suspects that in the past one of the main causes of unsatisfactory growth in the national income was inefficient managerial organization. The Cuban press has, for example, blamed the failure to achieve the ten-ton sugar harvest for 1970 by more than a million tons chiefly to inefficient management in the mills. This inefficiency lowered grinding capacity and sugar yields from the cane.[28]

28. See Premier Castro's trenchant analysis of the sugar harvest published in the weekly review in English of *Granma*, May 31, 1970. On July 21, the sugar produce was counted at 8,511,906 metric tons as reported in *Granma*, July 26, 1970, p. 5. (All subsequent references to *Granma* refer to its weekly review in English.)

Absenteeism in the Cuban firm remains a serious problem and there are increasing signs that centralized regimentation is filling the gap of frustrated expectations. Although *estímulo moral* has worked relatively well in mobilizing labor to solve the manpower shortage in the key agricultural harvest, the managerial performance under *estímulo moral* has not been convincing. Remarkable successes in a few sectors—sugar, to cite one in 1970—is often at the cost of setbacks or imbalances in other areas of production.

The exact characteristics of the current system and the degree to which the *pure* budgetary system has been embellished with Cuban additives are difficult to ascertain. The main sources that provided information on the debate are no longer in publication. All of them (e.g., *Cuba Socialista, Nuestra Industria: Revista Económica, Comercio Exterior*) disappeared between 1965 and 1967. Copies of the *Official Gazette* are difficult to obtain since the Cuban combine that controls publications and their exports (*Instituto Cubano del Libro*) has banned its export. But it is obvious that nonmarket (mobilization) means of allocating labor, socialization of the means of production, and moral incentives were further enhanced in 1967–68, and so was the office-like physical management of the firm without using either much private material incentives or monetary calculation. The Secretary of Organization of the Party, stated in late 1968: [29]

> How can we, under socialism, insure efficiency and the good organization and management of production? . . . Sometimes an attempt is made to apply the mechanism of economic control using the monetary procedure. We have rejected this mechanism and we want to go on leaving it aside; we do not want to measure efficiency by it. So how can we insure efficiency? . . . by organizing efficiency plans, pinpointing tasks, defining responsibilities, effectively controlling inventories, con-

29. Armando Hart Dávalos as reported in *Granma*, November 10, 1968, p. 2.

stantly concerning ourselves with the problems of maintenance. That is, we must go directly to the root of the problem, discarding monetary mechanisms, capitalist-type economic controls . . . technological skill must be applied in order to insure a centralized control especially in large industries . . .

The 1966–67 reforms emphasized the necessity of perfecting the administrative organization by improving technical efficiency. There was an attempt to enforce a large number of circulating capital norms down to the level of departments and shops.[30] Each was to be assigned fixed maximum finances for such capital items as inventories of raw materials, goods-in-process, finished products, and the number of days allowed for the collection of payments from customers. Methods of depreciation costing, previously neglected, were also emphasized during the period in question which also marked the trend back towards pure budgetary financing.

In practice, the application of self-finance during its heyday when it included close to one-third of Cuban enterprises was merely formal. It operated as a disguised or indirect version of budgetary financing. The essence of self-finance is responsibility for one's own financial survival. Yet firms on self-finance were bailed out; their deficits were covered by grants or "bank loans" that were not repayed; their expenditures were disconnected with their revenues. Thus "both kinds" of enterprises shared the same nature: they were managed like the typical government office. The Cuban manager, indeed, behaves like a government functionary. As in many countries, the choice of administrative functionaries often relies more heavily on political reliability than on technical expertise. The Cuban manager is a loyal political cadre first. This shows in his total monthly salary which is often below

30. See the report of the Vice-Ministry of Economics: "El análisis económico como instrumento de control del plan de eficiencia industrial," *Nuestra Industria: Revista Económica*, February, 1967, pp. 3–23.

that of his more technically qualified section chief; and it may sometimes be below his most skilled worker. As with government functionaries, his responsibilities are not very clearly specified since the Cuban firm does not have only one quantitative aim. Aside from achieving the highest physical output, the firm is expected to provide social activities among its members, upgrade skills, reduce technical costs, deepen consciousness and so on. This is in contrast to his market or business counterpart who is judged principally by his ability to improve the firm's profit performance. In the pursuit of this objective, the market manager is, by and large, empowered to hire the most productive workers he can find, and fire or transfer subordinates who are incompetent and unproductive. The Cuban manager, like the typical government functionary, does not have as much power. His power to hire is subject to the consent of his industrial ministry and the Ministry of Labor and the latter's regional office. His power to fire and transfer workers is subject to veto by the party nucleus in each firm and, to a lesser extent, by union leaders and members of his administrative staff, and by the relevant ministry.

CHAPTER THREE

Moral Stimulation
as a Non-Wage System
of Labor Allocation

Moral Incentives and the Labor Market

In this chapter we probe further the allocative mechanism of moral incentives as its operation in the more fascinating human area of labor allocation is described. As the analysis develops, the reader might appreciate the appropriateness of the term "moral stimulation," since the mechanism of moral incentives in either Cuba, China or North Korea * is not a completely spontaneous process. It is channeled from above by the many organizations—which are really sub-organizations of the Party—into a widespread competition for official honors and social approval among the masses below. A great deal of psychological pressure is used by the activist leaders and organizations to get people to "volunteer" their services without direct administrative coercion. And the mechanism of moral incentives is merely one major aspect of the nonmarket system of labor allocation. The other is administrative assignment of laborers to their various places of employment. For these reasons, the term "moral stimulation" seems more appropriate than "moral incentives;" the latter suggests a completely spontaneous process of behavior. But I shall take the Cuban and Chinese leaders' name for

* The reference here is to the later's "Daean" work system.

their distinctive allocating mechanism and have thus used the phrase "moral incentives" liberally in this work. Moral behavior is understood neutrally as one defined by a group as moral; moreover the phrase "moral incentives" refers to a nonmonetary means of achieving a goal of whatever kind. Ideally, moral incentives is viewed by the Cuban leaders as a work attitude consisting in the internalized learning of voluntarily working more heavily for the community's profit and relatively less for one's private interests, including material ones.

Of course there is much administrative assignment of labor into so-called voluntary work projects. In practice it is not easy to distinguish between the two kinds of labor allocation above. However, the latter difficulty is insufficient ground for denying field reports of many observers that much labor in Cuba is allocated decentrally without direct administrative coercion through the nonwage system of moral incentives, or what the Cubans also call *conciencia* and *espíritu comunista*—especially among the young and activist workers.

The mechanism of moral incentives is viewed by its practitioners in Cuba and China as a way of implementing the communist egalitarian rule of "from each according to his ability, to each according to his need." However they realize that this rule is being implemented in an important way under conditions of material and cultural backwardness; whence the interesting and novel features of that rule as it is embodied in the system of giving nonmonetary symbols of social approval in exchange for acts of production—mainly voluntary labor including the acceptance of wage reductions. I shall argue that the primary reliance on moral incentives implies the elimination of the labor market and its mode of exchanging monetary awards for acts of production. From a strict logical point of view the comprehensive use of moral incentives is compatible with the labor market. One can argue that moral incentives merely changes the workers' atttiudes. We know that as attitude towards work changes, so do wage rates, all other influences being held constant. Thus the now severely narrow wage differentials of post-1966 Cuba and China may still *retain* the same amount of, and *attract* additional man-hours because of the workers' greater love of, or lesser aversion for work. Although workers may not receive the monetary value of their contributions to production, the new and progressively more egalitarian wage differentials could still reflect the relative private disutilities (costs) of workers. The argument is sound but stretches the concept of the market to its logical limit, and is not the actual labor market of experience. In order to *retain* (reduce) current supplies of workers and to continue to attract (repel) potential entrants, money wages adjust upwards (downwards) in actual market societies. This is not so in Cuba and China where wages are fixed arbitrarily for long periods and the burden of adjusting workers to a new more egalitarian wage is placed on nonmonetary awards.

A nation relying primarily on moral incentives must abolish primary reliance on the monetary incentive system which awards workers in proportion to the realized monetary values of their contributions to production. The last sentence seems true logically as well as empirically in Cuba and China, particularly after 1966. Policy in the two countries oscillated on the desirable mix between monetary and non-monetary incentives. In Cuba, Guevara introduced it gradually in his then monolithic Ministry of Industries and in the various volunteer work projects, particularly in agriculture, in 1960. Partial concessions to the greater use of material incentives were made during his incumbency in connection with the new wage scales and piece rates devised in 1962 and 1963 and subsequently implemented. Mesa-Lago, whose work is cited here, first published this complete series of wage scales which showed (up to the mid-1960's) higher wage differentials than now exist. In practice, money income differentials were made effectively smaller by an equalitarian physical distribution of most consumer goods and the provision of demonetized, "free" services. But since 1966 Cuba and China renewed and redoubled their efforts in institutionalizing the mechanism of moral incentives. This was often described as constructing the "new man" whose defining quality was his community awareness and readiness to sacrifice private interests. Money wage differentials still exist, of course. But monetary incentives, although they still play an important role, are of secondary allocative importance. The sign that monetary incentives are of secondary importance is the abolition of the labor market.

Moral incentives is thus a nonmarket decentralist mode of resource allocation based on feelings of group solidarity; it is manifested in the socially approved competition for social status based on prizes and titles of all kinds. By this is not meant that comprehensively decentralist distribution of labor; administrative assignment of labor is much practiced in Cuba and China. Since 1960 the Cuban Labor Ministry and its regional office formally took charge of labor allocation and Law 1225 of September, 1969 forcefully reasserted this early formal feature of Cuban socialism. Hence allocation by means of the offer of symbolic awards in exchange for work is only a partial substitute for the absent labor market; the other substitute is administrative assignment of labor. But here, too, moral stimulation of the worker, combined with informal bargaining between administrators and workers and their various organizations, blunts the bias towards coercive administrative direction.

We shall deal with the changes that came about from the time of the introduction of moral stimulation in Cuba in 1960 to what was the policy's fullest culmination in 1970. However, we might first note previous discussions of the mechanism of moral incentives.[1] James O'Connor interprets the Cuban *estímulo moral* to mean the same thing as "social incentives" since, according to him, the former concept covers activity which is "economically disinterested" thus conforming "to Marx's original idea of emulation under socialism."[2] Paul Sweezy and Leo Huberman, in their discussion of the distinction between moral versus material incentives, concluded that the phrase "collective incentives" is a more appropriate rendering of the meaning of "moral incentives." They add that "material incentives" is more accurately denoted by "private incentives." Thus, they would replace the expression "moral versus material incentives" with "collective versus private incentives" since in both "material gains are envisaged: the opposition lies rather in the composition of the gains and the way they are distributed."[3] Their definition overemphasizes the egalitarian aim of the mechanism of moral incentives. Like O'Connor's, it seems to be reductionist on grounds that moral stimulation as a goal is a complex one consisting of several subgoals of which an egalitarian productive structure is one. Sweezy and Huberman emphasize this one aspect rather unduly when they state that the nature of the system of moral incentives consists essentially in reward-

1. For alternative earlier treatments of this topic, see my "Moral Stimulation as a Nonmarket Mode of Labor Allocation in Cuba," *Studies in Comparative International Development*, Vol. 6 (1970–71) No. 6; Carmelo Mesa-Lago, *The Labor Sector and Socialist Distribution in Cuba* (New York: Praeger, 1968). In the Chinese context, Charles Hoffman's works, though in need of updating, are definitive. His book is cited later and its argument summarized in his "Work Incentives in Chinese Industry and Agriculture," in *An Economic Profile of Mainland China: Studies Prepared for the Joint Economic Committee, Congress of the United States.* (Washington, D.C.: U.S. Government Printing Office, 1967) Vol. 2. In the Korean context, Kim Byong Sik, *Modern Korea* (New York: International, 1970).

2. James O'Connor, "The Organized Working Class in the Cuban Revolution," *Studies on the Left*, March–April, 1966, p. 25.

3. Their editorial in *Monthly Review*, November, 1967, p. 14.

ing workers collectively through the increased production of such public goods as communal kitchens, buses, education, and public health. In this view, the empirical measure of the success of moral stimulation is decided by noting the shift in the structure of production and consumption in favor of goods of a public nature in contrast to privately consumed production such as automobiles. On this view, Cuban society certainly has radically altered the structure of national consumption in favor of collective consumption as Sweezy and Huberman have documented in their latest work on Cuba.[4] The view presented here is slightly different; we can view the mechanism of moral incentives independently of any or all of its major goals. This view of the matter consists of seeing that mechanism as a substitute for the labor market. Indeed, the Cuban leaders often contrast the mechanism of moral incentives to the pre-revolutionary system of labor allocation by means of the market. In referring to the capitalist labor market they use such labels as "cruel system of wages and hunger." The market wages system is regarded as "immoral" and as a disguised form of "slavery."

In the system of moral incentives, on the other hand, every eligible person is assured a job and the principal means of payment and allocation of workers to their various uses is not money but nonmonetary awards. Thus, from the organizational point of view, the term "monetary versus nonmonetary" is more accurate than Sweezy's "private versus collective" incentives; and it is also more accurate than the term "material versus moral incentives," which is the phrase most often employed in the literature on the subject.

The preference for nonmarket methods in the allocation of productive staff is bound up with the goal of instilling a new work ethic in which workers, including managers, are internally motivated to work for the net social good including

4. Leo Huberman and Paul Sweezy, *Socialism in Cuba* (New York: Monthly Review, 1969).

the individual's. Insofar as this goal is achieved, it forms the decentralized or voluntary aspect of the system of moral incentives. The planners regard the general willingness to earn moral or social titles as evidence of the worker's desire to serve society including himself. From an organizational perspective what is interesting about this aspect of the Cuban social system is the manner and the extent to which workers and managers are motivated to compete for titles of sociomoral distinction and how this has replaced the market wages system of attracting workers by means of large variations in monetary and material rewards. Needless to say, the competition for nonmonetary rewards must be instituted or taught for it to function in a workable manner.

We might mention briefly the various agencies and ways by which a significant portion of the citizenry is taught to respond to nonmonetary rewards. Workers were motivated and informed through the educational system, the media, the Party, and the creatively energetic publicity department of the Commission of Revolutionary Orientation, to value titles of various social ranks. The Commission is composed of teams of writers, sociologists, designers and other experts who coordinate the state's publicity efforts, and inform and exhort the population mainly in matters regarding the production and labor needs of agriculture and industry. The titles or claims to social rank that the worker may compete for are myriad. Titles vary from public praise by the leaders to medals, buttons, diplomas, plaques, certificates of communist work, and honorable mentions in factory bulletins. Other rewards include banners such as the May Day, Hundred Years of Struggle, Heroes of Moncada, and Heroic Guerrilla Awards; election by the worker's peers to the mass advance-guard movement which included some 235,000 people by late May, 1969; election to the even higher-ranking Communist Party; an appearance with Fidel Castro or another high official in the local *Plaza de la Revolución;* the yearly Hero of Labor—the highest prize to which one can aspire—and many others. And we might also include titles in a job or organization as parts of the nonmonetary incentive system; these have increased in quantity. In the 40,000-strong Youth Centennial Column which cut cane in the 1970 harvest, there were 292 brigade leaders. Some nonmonetary awards (prizes) are won individually, some collectively, examples of which were the gold medals for individuals who cut 2500 pounds of sugarcane in the 1970 harvest and the "millionaire" brigades, respectively. Some prizes won collectively such as the Hero of Moncada banner had to be defended periodically for the right to fly it. Some prizes confer modest material benefits like vacations and pensions; but these hybrid prizes are negligible. And in the institutionalization of prizes, there are large public ceremonies several times a year in which workers who respond to nonmonetary rewards are feted and honored for public emulation.

An institution for enlisting worker participation in the process of working for nonmonetary rewards is the latter's participation in electing individual and group winners to the advance-guard movement. The worker does this in emulation assemblies called in each brigade or work center—the fundamental units of production. Since January, 1966 this decentralized procedure of awarding a prize or title has been simplified and only a minimum set of requirements have to be met by aspirants to the title of vanguard worker. There are also task-oriented groups encountered in units of production, usually on Saturdays, to discuss work problems and increase output. Finally, other mass organizations, most importantly the ubiquitous block committees (CDR*), all led by the Communist Party, employ subtle psychological and other pressures to actively induce workers to respond to nonmonetary rewards.

Why do the leaders rely so heavily on moral prizes as

* *Comités para la defensa de la Revolución.*

incentives for additional man-hours? The skeptic's answer is that this is a cheap way to increase effort, what with the current state of austerity and consumer rationing. Surely, the main leaders appreciate an alternative to material means of increasing the supply of labor. Yet an obsessional hatred for the market and for its companion institutions of money and material incentives was present in the passionate commitment to promote the "communist spirit," This doctrine is interpreted by the leaders to mean "from each according to his ability and to each according to his need" and, to the extent that workers responded to moral incentives, the mode of labor deployment and remuneration in the system of moral stimulation implemented the communist distributive principle.

The relentless pursuit of egalitarianism was dramatically reemphasized on July 26, 1969 by Fidel Castro: ". . . the Revolution aspires—as one of the steps toward communism—to equalize incomes from the bottom up, for all workers, regardless of the type of work they do." In the same speech, he renewed his promise to eventually eliminate money and its progressive reduction at the present time to a mere aid in the distribution of consumer goods. Money wages still play an important role in motivating workers for additional effort but this function is of secondary importance to moral incentives. The influence of the Marxian anti-market theory of alienation reminiscent of Marx's *Economic and Philosophical Manuscripts* of 1844 is clearly evident.

Socialist Emulation

Of all the various methods employed for institutionalizing moral incentives, the implementation of socialist emulation stands out as a principal one. Although ideally, moral stimulation was meant to be as decentralist as possible, in the past it has been blemished by bureaucracy and some coercion by administrators is charge of organizing emulation among workers. And in the past, the use of what has been called here hybrid prizes (because cash and goods were mixed with the moral prize) was widespread. But the administration of socialist emulation has been progressively improved and simplified to come closer to the ideal standard, thanks to the work of the Committees For The Struggle Against Bureaucracy and others. The main function of the administration of socialist emulation is the setting of rules and prizes governing the competition for prizes. Competition was to be fraternal marked by nonsecrecy, a spirit of camaraderie about the whole process and willingness to share one's superior method. Fraternal competition takes place among individuals and groups, for example, among brigades, sections, factories, regions and the like. In addition there are *ad hoc* and task-oriented emulations which are either permanent or merely temporary and which disband as soon as the specific work is over and which in the past several years have increasingly made use of historic dates—such as emulations on the anniversary of the Bay of Pigs invasion or Che Guevara's death. Like the ubiquitous party cadres in each work center, the administrators of socialist emulation translate into day-to-day practice what is asserted by the official ideology urging that all citizens and students "be taught the value of emulative work and the difference between capitalism and socialism as being based on the difference between competition for private gain and emulation for the sake of increasing the output of the community." [5]

The principal aim of the administrators of the complex system of socialist emulation is to increase the supply of labor and skills in various sectors while guiding their deployment according to the Plan's social priorities. They execute this function by setting up elaborate schemes of work norms and by devising a rich variety of moral titles for fulfillment and

5. From the official report by the Cuban government to the UNESCO Conference on Education and Social Development held in Santiago, Chile in 1962.

overfulfillment of norms. They as well as the Party are charged with the active promotion of the advance-guard or vanguard movement. Since 1968 only the overfulfillment of certain norms was required for election into the vanguard movement. Although material rewards are still given, rewards are now moral titles which bestow public praise and social status on its recipients. Workers are urged to compete for and earn moral prizes in exchange for work. In place of the old market system of responding to a scale of differential prices for labor, workers are taught to respond mainly to a scale of moral titles or prizes of different social ranks. The greater is the worker's effort and improvement of his skills, the higher is the social grade of the prize he receives. Moral prizes are given also in exchange for direct voluntary and overtime labor. In regard to material awards for emulation during the 1966 sugar harvest, only 1.7 percent of some 300,000 workers who participated in the emulation plans received material awards. Since "the number of material awards is small, they continue to occupy a secondary place in the emulation system."[6] Material stimuli included cash but a clear ideological preference exists for goods in kind like refrigerators, televisions, motorcycles, housing, vacations, and travel to Eastern Europe. In late 1965 and early 1966 cash prizes were abolished.[7] The honor, communitarian, and play motives in the system of moral incentives were encouraged. The play motive is found, for example, in the festival-like voluntary work projects in agriculture. In contrast, Soviet Stakhanovism uses material bonuses heavily for stimulating workers to fulfill and overfulfill work quotas. It seems better from the logical point of view, to regard material stimuli associated with prizes as part of the wage system still used in a very limited form in Cuba. These material awards, after all, increase real shares of workers in national income and are part of the

6. C. Mesa-Lago, *The Labor Sector* . . . , p. 141.
7. *Granma*, December 12, 1965, p. 6.

material incentive system still used. But although wages in money and in kind are still paid workers, I shall explain later why wages in Cuba are not the main means by which current labor resources are allocated.

The administration of socialist emulation was lodged in the Ministry of Labor but the latter's branches reached out into the various ministries and enterprises. This was so since 1962. The Ministry of Labor took it over to systematize evaluative criteria for success in the various emulation campaigns and plans. Excessive bureaucracy characterized this early period: between January and April, 1962, there were some 13,000 emulation commissions doing work in every nook and cranny of the administrative planning structure.[8] Part of their job was the enlisting of workers into emulation plans, devising prizes, collecting and processing candidates, etc. With a great show of effort the Ministry of Labor completed a study in late 1962 and published its findings in a document titled, "Project to Regulate The Organization of Socialist Emulation."[9] This document marks the institutionalization of socialist emulation. It acknowledged that "until now socialist emulation has not yet acquired its proper content. The main cause of this was that the mass of workers did not participate directly in the emulation program and hence it was characterized by bureaucracy."[10]

The document called for the founding of a National Emulation Commission to coordinate all of the various efforts of relatively decentralized emulation agencies in implementing the rules for emulation, but one of its chief accomplishments was the elaboration of criteria for evaluating successful emulators. We need not go into the various organizations which composed this nation-wide commission; as was ex-

8. C. Mesa-Lago, *The Labor Sector* . . . , Chapter V.
9. *Gaceta Oficial de la República de Cuba* (hereafter, *Gaceta Oficial*), February 7, 1963.
10. Ibid., p. 1401.

pected, the important national organizations and ministries were represented. An Executive Committee For Emulation was set up, presided over by the Ministry of Labor, and so were provincial-regional and local emulation commissions dominated by the Labor Ministry.

Each trust (consolidated enterprise) had its own emulation office and disaggregated the indices laid down by the Executive Committee with the approval of the National Commission. These indices pertained to

   a) Control of each worker's tasks, *including quality control.*
   b) Monthly control of basic materials cost for such items as metal, wood, fuel, cotton, auxiliary materials . . .
   c) Daily control of attendance and punctuality.

The shop section of the National Trade Union (CTC-R)* will oversee and be responsible for implementation of these organizational measures . . . In case management fails in complying with these measures, the labor union section is obliged to denounce it so that superior bodies may take the appropriate disciplinary measures.

The following were some of the rules issued and were characteristic. On the evaluation of the plan or work:

Individual Emulation

One hundred points are given for fulfilling the plan or work task and three points are given for every percent of overfulfillment. Six points are deducted for every percent of underfulfillment.

Collective Emulation

The valuation of the [plan] index is the same for Collective Emulation.

Similar rules were designed for five additional success indicators for savings, quality, assistance and punctuality, pro-

* Confederación de trabajadores cubanos—Revolucionaria.

fessional improvement, and number of individual participants in the emulation plans. The general rule for measuring the index—which was spelled out in detail by the various local and enterprise emulation committees—was given as follows:

Industrial Emulation

Satisfactory work performance is measured by work of a 100 percent quality and 100 points are given for such work. Five points are deducted for each percent of low quality—a sign of inadequate work performance.

Collective Emulation

The valuation of this index is the same for Collective Emulation.[11]

The best workers for the trimester, semester, or yearly check-ups were those who accumulated the largest number of points. Note that the points system used in the emulation program was a kind of pricing system which reflected the different relative utilities of the various indices to the central policymakers. In evaluating the progress of emulation plans, the assembly from each work center met every month for that purpose; on the enterprise level, every trimester; on the ministerial level, every semester. The National Emulation Commission met at least once every trimester and it chose the yearly winner of the Hero of Labor award [12]—after 1966 multiple awards were authorized—from the best vanguard workers chosen by lower-level agencies. With respect to the composition of the moral stimuli, the following were listed: pennants, medals, buttons of all varieties; honorable mentions in the work center's book of honor and its bulletin board. With respect to the award of memberships in the advance-guard movement, a worker was awarded that title from each

11. These and the preceding quotes are from *Gaceta Oficial*, p. 1402.
12. Ibid., pp. 1403–1404.

work unit, profession, enterprise, ministry, region, province, or other national body. A significant part of socialist emulation at this time was the list of material prizes such as cash awards consisting of 75 percent of the worker's pay upon his election as the consolidated enterprise's vanguard worker. At the unit level, a cash award of 25 to 50 percent was given. Other material awards included paid vacations and travel but material awards were, in general, of secondary importance to the awarding of moral titles. Later, the former were reduced even more during the higher stage of development of moral stimulation as a whole, including socialist emulation—its "non-individualistic and non-bureaucratic mass stage."

Officials in the administrative hierarchy not only enlist workers in the various emulation plans but they are charged as well with the task of encouraging voluntary labor donations during weekends, holidays, and vacations, and after the standard work hours. In enlisting workers in the emulation plans, including those for volunteer labor, some form of coercion was occasionally used in spite of the professed ideal of making the system of moral incentives as voluntary as possible. During the acknowledged "individualistic and bureaucratic" stage of socialist emulation, particularly for some time after early 1963, workers at production meetings were often pressured to subscribe to the emulation plans, including voluntary labor (the latter is recorded in the worker's labor identity booklet). Emulation contracts thus publicly obtained were indeed required for submission to the relevant emulation commission of the unit of production although the legal rule frowned on the use of coercion.[13]

In January, 1966, a decisive reform in the institution of socialist emulation called for the abolition of enforced emulation contracts. A leading planner, in comparing this new

13. See "Reglamento Para La Organización De La Emulación," Article 53, in the government's *Gaceta Oficial*, May 21, 1964.

"non-bureaucratic mass stage" to the previous structure, described the latter as one ridden by

> an extraordinary rigidity . . . . Second: An extraordinarily ex-
> cessive number of indices . . . . Third: formal selection in as-
> semblies in which the masses did not participate, in which the
> pre-set norms of emulation commissions dominated the general
> and inflexible practice which resulted in the bureaucratization
> of all emulation . . .[14]

Cash awards were reduced in number and size in favor of
goods in kind. The myriad numbers of emulation commissions
in lower levels of production were severely reduced in number and scheduled for elimination, thus saving greatly on
skilled personnel. The plethora of indices were drastically
reduced in number to the fulfillment of the work plan, rational
utilization of raw materials, professional improvement, attendance, and contributions of voluntary labor. Only minimum acceptable standards of these indicators had to be met
for winning the title of vanguard worker. The secretaries of
the Party nucleus and the labor union together with the ad-
ministrator of the work center determined which individuals
and groups met these minima; workers in full assembly elected
vanguards from the proposed candidates.

Finally, in the second half of 1968, a further refinement
in the workings of socialist emulation was introduced. Prizes
were tailored to suit the average worker so that the wider
masses might regard them as being within reach of their capa-
bilities. Norms were further reduced to overfulfillment of the
plan, full attendance and punctuality, voluntary labor, re-
nunciation of overtime pay, and interest in the social life of
the work center. Finally, in the words of Miguel Martín, who
heads the National Trade Union, "only those material incentives of a social nature will be used." [15] The gradual elimina-

14. Basilio Rodríguez, "Las nuevas normas de la emulación socialista," *Cuba Socialista*, April, 1966, pp. 95–97.

15. Miguel Martín, "The Development of Proletarian Consciousness," *Granma*, October 1, 1968, p. 2.

tion of overtime pay began in the second semester of 1967. In the second half of 1969, this campaign to make overtime work voluntary has met with success as we shall have occasion to note again later. In the past several years as well, there was a gradual return to time payments in contrast to the complicated piece-work system previously in force. Although, as we shall see, other pragmatic reasons for this change were present, it was rightly noted that time payments were more in keeping with moral stimulation. A significant reform of the institution of socialist emulation since 1966 took the form of emulation based on "historic dates" about which some examples will be cited later. By late 1969 it seems to have become institutionalized into a mass movement emphasizing group solidarity and minimal bureaucratic forms. Its significance for the issue of relative decentralization was expressed this way by one of the highest ranking officials: "emulation . . . has assumed a different . . . meaning, changing from the bureaucratic and administrative emulation which it was before to an emulation based on historical dates . . ." [16]

Administrative Allocation

We now come to the other labor allocating substitute for the absent labor market. Labor is partially centrally allocated chiefly through the Ministry of Labor and its regional office, but also by the army. A law passed in March, 1960 gave the Ministry of Labor power to freeze and set wages. This was followed the following month by a decree obliging employers, workers, and the self-employed to register their qualifications in order to obtain jobs in conformance with the rules of the ministry's Labor Control Office.[17] The labor

16. Armando Hart Dávalos in *Granma*, September 28, 1969, p. 4. A recent historic addition is the *Jornada Guerrillera* in honor of Che Guevara and Camilo Cienfuegos extending from October 8 to 28.

17. *Hispanic American Report*, June, 1960, Vol. 13, No. 4, p. 240.

ministry since then gradually acquired stronger powers over labor distribution culminating in 1962 with the introduction of the worker's identity card (*carnet laboral*).[18] This fourteen-page booklet became a requirement for obtaining work in the state sector; it contained records of place of employment, type of work performed, attendance and punctuality, volunteer labor, and work speed and political attitudes. It is not necessary to go through a detailed history of how the labor ministry acquired increasingly larger allocative powers except to note that in practice it did not assert its powers strongly in the early years of Cuban socialism. With the start of the massive investment strategy of 1966 and the concomitant growing complexity in labor allocation, its planning role has been increased.

In the allocation of workers to their competing uses, the Ministry of Labor may obtain assistance from other agencies. A case in point took place in early 1968 when the ministry ruled more than 60,000 current jobs for women only. Commissions made up of members of the Cuban Women's Federation (FMC) by April 30 had interviewed 31,187 of the men holding these jobs to arrange for their reallocation to agricultural and more arduous tasks. "Once a worker is interviewed by the FMC Commission, he is again interviewed at the Ministry of Labor after which he chooses a new job according to his vocation, education, trade, etc., and the need for manpower in various areas throughout the country." [19] The report went on to note that the majority of those interviewed expressed satisfaction with the measure. A somewhat more decentralized administrative technique is used in staffing local and small-scale enterprises. In the latest massive expropriation

18. Law No. 1021, Articles 14 and 15, *Gaceta Oficial*, May 4, 1962; also Law No. 696, February 22, 1960; Law No. 761, Article 1, March 21, 1960; Law No. 907, Article 21, December 21, 1960. A detailed account is in Cuban Economic Research Project, *Labor Conditions in Communist Cuba* (Coral Gables: University of Miami Press, 1963).

19. *Granma*, May 5, 1968, p. 1.

of the remaining small private businesses in March, 1968,
which saw the nonagricultural sector nearly completely socialized, the staffing of these 57,600 firms was supervised by
and came chiefly from the Committees for the Defense of
the Revolution (CDR) in consultation with such others as
the Ministry of Labor, the Communist Party, the FMC, the
CTC-R and so on.[20]

In some professions, a compulsory service of three years
was required. Thus, new medical and dental graduates were
to serve three years in the rural areas where these professions
were notoriously absent in the pre-revolutionary period. Here,
the Rural Medical Service of the Ministry of Public Health
was in charge—a practice that had its beginnings in 1960. This
rule has been increasingly applied subsequently, full-time
private practice having been abolished in 1964.[21] The same
length of service in the army was instituted in November,
1963 for those over seventeen and in particular, for juvenile
delinquents and other such "aimless loafers." This measure may
have been partly due to the marked drop in agricultural labor
first badly felt in 1961 and the uncertainties and lack of training of the temporary volunteer brigades that flowed from
the urban centers for the harvest season. The army at this
time was divided into two major groups: soldiers and workers.
The latter devoted most of their time to the sugar harvest and
the coffee crop as well as other tasks. But the army soldiers
also devoted a portion of their time to agricultural work. At
the time this method of labor deployment was adopted, the
leadership announced that it would be a great source of savings, since the men would be paid a very low nominal
wage.[22] The famous Che Guevara Trailblazer Brigade formed

20. *Granma*, April 7, 1968, p. 3; May 12, 1968, p. 2.
21. Cuban Economic Research Project, *Social Security in Communist Cuba* (Coral Gables: University of Miami Press, 1964), pp.
250–52.
22. Cf. Theodore Draper, *Castroism, Theory and Practice* (New
York: Praeger, 1965), pp. 174–76.

in late 1967 is just one illustration of the significant use of the military for construction, roadbuilding, and land clearing. It is led by officers of the Rebel Army, manned chiefly by soldiers, and has a military-type organization.[23] The equally renowned Youth Centennial Column was organized in a similar fashion in 1968; it is semi-military, too, in the sense that the three-year recruits may serve their three-year military draft there instead. Although they performed productive work, they trained militarily as well and wore uniforms. The trend towards the militarization of work received new impetus in 1968 with the organization during the harvest season of voluntary labor and industry on the civil defense pattern.

On the disincentive side, moral stimulation as a nonmarket mode of labor allocation employs a complex scheme of penalties for work laxity including vagrancy—which is illegal. Since practically every person is assured of a job, the whip of starvation for lack of work—begging, for instance, has disappeared—is absent. Administrative and other nonmarket counterparts to that whip of the wage system were devised which sometimes resulted in an unexpected measure of "regimentation."[24] For example, as countermeasures to lateness, absenteeism, and negligence, the Minister of Industries in 1961 was constrained to propose "compulsory measures . . . to sustain production."[25] According to him, lateness and absenteeism that year reached "alarming characteristics." Proportional monetary wage reductions were enacted for failure to achieve the work quota. In the First National Conference On Emulation in early 1964, the Minister of Labor proposed measures for meting out public blame for the laziest workers in the form of posters to be displayed in the shop and factory

23. *Granma*, November 12, 1967, p. 1.
24. E.g., L. Huberman and P. Sweezy, *Socialism in Cuba*, chapter 8.
25. Che Guevara, *Revolución*, Sept. 25, 1961 and April 16, 1962.

with descriptions of the workers' errors.[26] In other cases, punishment takes the form of inter-plant, inter-enterprise or inter-regional transfer—depending on the severity of the work misdemeanor. In more serious cases, managers and workers could theoretically be suspended from five to thirty days or sent to serve from "one to twelve months in the Center of Rehabilitation at Guanahacabibes," a corrective labor camp set up at the initiative of the Minister of Industries.[27] There was a mounting movement towards stricter disciplinary measures as insubordination, negligence, lateness, and absenteeism mounted.[28] A law which took effect on January 1, 1965, authorized, among other measures, transfers to less desirable work centers and outright dismissal from the job in serious cases.[29] To discourage persons and workers from a noted tendency in 1962 towards theft, robbery, and swindling of state property, the well-known law 1098 in 1963 meted out harsh jail sentences for these offenses;[30] but in practice, the law does not seem to have been significantly enforced.

Function of Wage Differences

If a labor market is effectively absent as the main labor allocator, what social function do the limited wage differences perform? In answering this intriguing and important question, I should first like to describe the Cuban wage schemes to see what general principles emerge from our inquiry into their various functions.

In the following account, the distinction needs to be

26. A. Martínez Sánchez, *El Mundo,* March 6, 1964, pp. 1–2.

27. *Nuestra Industria* (Journal of the Ministry of Industries), March, 1962, p. 44; its article on "Administrative Disciplinary Commission," issue of February, 1964, pp. 75–76; title translated by the present writer into English.

28. B. Rodríguez in *Cuba Socialista,* October, 1966, pp. 143–55.

29. *Revolución,* October 3, 1964 on "Ley de Justicia Laboral."

30. *Granma,* May 11, 1969.

drawn between the theory of official publications and the reality of Cuban practice. We saw that the wages inherited from the capitalist period were frozen. Then in 1962–63 the new system of "wage scales and work norms" was painstakingly adopted from Soviet manuals and soon implemented, as it was in China. In fact, there was confusion in the implementation of the new wage policy, although Cuban officials claim actual completion of the process of introducing the new wage policy by late 1964 and early 1965.[31] In late 1966 and early 1967, there was a gradual reversal of policy in favor of straight time payments and a severe narrowing of the moderately wide salary differentials of the new wage scales.

The wage system of the mid-1960's was based on four main scales each with their seven or eight wage grades based on skill differences. These four main wage scales—agricultural, nonagricultural, administrative, techno-managerial— were subdivided into seven or eight categories of levels of technical skills; the nonagricultural scale was also classified in three categories of work conditions—average, harmful, and extremely arduous. The total wage corresponding to each technical grade of a particular salary scale was based on a time-consuming motion and time study of the work process itself, on pieces of work done by the average laborer in a grade per unit of time measured in hours or work-days. This was so since there was not only a basic hourly salary but rewards for overfulfilling quotas as well.

The nonagricultural scale gradually introduced in the second semester of 1963 was this:

GROUP	I	II	III	IV	V	VI	VII	VIII
HOURLY WAGE (in pesos)	.48	.56	.65	.76	.89	1.05	1.23	1.45

The schedule was designed so that the minimum wage per month would amount to 85 pesos for a six day week; 72.4 percent of the nonagricultural labor force was placed in the first

31. C. Mesa-Lago, *The Labor Sector* . . . , p. 181.

three technical grades. Thus although the eighth grade was three times as large as the minimum hourly wage for unskilled labor, 70 percent of the workers earned a basic salary ranging from 85 to 115 pesos a month,[32] for average or normal work conditions; for harmful work and extremely arduous tasks they were uniformly raised by 20 and 35 percent, respectively. In the agricultural scale introduced a year later there were seven technical grades and just one normal category of labor conditions reflecting the relative simplicity of agricultural tasks.[33]

AGRICULTURAL SCALE	1	2	3	4	5	6	7	8
(in pesos)	.37	.42	.48	.56	.65	.76	.88	None

Note its contrast with the industrial (nonagricultural) scale; the different rates were less below those for industry than it was previously. Agricultural wages were improved relative to industry to reverse the mass exodus of workers from agriculture, first acutely felt in 1961. The salary scale for administrative employees released in mid-1963 contained eight grades but salary rates were by the month since there were no adequate means for measuring their outputs. These salaries in pesos correspond to the eight grades: 85; 98.60; 114.75; 134.30; 157.25; 185.30; 218.45; 263.50. Due to the scantiness of the available sources and partial official secrecy, we do not know for certain whether administrative salaries were divided into grades of skills. Also, we do not have official data on the techno-managerial scale.[34] Field observers, however, give

32. A. Martínez-Sánchez, "La implantación del nuevo sistema salarial en las industrias de Cuba," *Cuba Socialista*, October, 1963, p. 10. The peso was worth a U.S. dollar prior to 1959; the current rate in free exchanges ranges from $0.30 to $0.10 according to Dr. Mesa-Lago, *The Labor Sector* . . . ., p. xix.

33. I. Talavera and H. R. Herrera, "La organización del trabajo y el salario en la agricultura," *Cuba Socialista*, May–June, 1965, p. 70.

34. See C. Mesa-Lago, *The Labor Sector* . . . , pp. 99–101.

the impression that managers are paid like government functionaries who earn fixed salaries of about 200 to 250 pesos.[35]
Although the manager usually earns more than most skilled
workers, he may often earn less.

A minimum agricultural wage of 60 pesos per month, 69
pesos for state farm workers, and 85 pesos in urban work
centers prevailed at this time. Agricultural wages have been
raised to equal those in industry and the effective actual minimum is about 95 pesos a month. The maximum legal wage is
450 pesos while the current minimum legal wage is 85.[36] High-
ranking government officials are exempt from the legal ceiling,
cabinet ministers earning about 700 pesos. New appointments
of more than 300 pesos were avoided as much as possible.
The system of scales and hourly rates corresponding to each
of the many grades within the scale in question suggests one
major principle of Cuban wage formation—the long-run
material encouragement of the formation of badly needed
technical skills. This can be regarded, if we like, as a future
allocative function since its purpose is to attract students to
enter the technical professions and encourage workers to upgrade their skills by enrolling in technical courses. We are
concerned, however, with the proper allocative role of wage
differences—the allocation of workers to their various uses
in the current period.

In regard to the allocative role of wages in the current
period, one cannot regard the wages just described as market
wages. Their range of variation is severely limited from
roughly 95 to 450 pesos and by the practice of avoiding giving the higher hourly wages corresponding to the higher technical grades. In part the latter practice is due to the fact that

35. Anthony Sylvester, "East Europeans in Cuba," *East Europe*,
October, 1965, p. 7. Also, Maurice Zeitlin, "Inside Cuba: Workers and
Revolution," *Ramparts*, March, 1970.

36. Michael Frayn in his "Cuba Today," *The Globe and Mail*
(Toronto), January 14, 1969.

41.9 and 42.6 percent of the total labor force of 2,198,000 in 1963 were agricultural and nonagricultural respectively, and only 10.7 and 4.8 percent were administrative and techno-managerial.[37] In addition, wages bore no systematic relationship to the scarcity of job specifications. But the other major reason for claiming that Cuban wages were not market allocators is that money wage incomes could not be realized in the consumer goods sector. Most consumer goods since late 1960 and early 1961 were physically rationed according to some austere criterion of individual need at fixed nominal prices. In practice, of course, there operated an insignificant labor market in the illegal practice of norm juggling in order to attract workers from other places at closer to their scarcity price. But this was denounced as labor piracy and, since the mid-1960's, has not been a serious problem—what with greater administrative supervision of labor mobility. Also, some part of the nominal wage differences could be realized in the few legal places such as restaurants, and in the semi-legal treks to the countryside for food, where the worker could buy items at close to their scarcity values.[38] The insignificant current allocative role of wages affect their ability to allocate future workers to the various occupations. And it also makes its incentive role a minor one.

To strengthen the secondary incentive role of wage differences in given jobs—which the worker inherited from the capitalist period, or he chose on other grounds, or to which he was assigned—an elaborate system of piecework was combined with the salary scales. (Group piecework was applied to work of a joint or team nature such as construction.) The

37. Max Nolff in Dudley Seers, ed., *Cuba, the Economic and Social Revolution* (Chapel Hill: University of North Carolina Press, 1964), p. 317.

38. Buying directly from peasants is illegal but overlooked if the amounts involved are not big enough to suggest an organized business; the peasants, however, prefer to barter rather than sell for increasingly unspendable money.

worker's hourly wage was made conditional on work done by a rule to fulfill a minimum quota or norm as a pre-condition for receiving his basic hourly wage. This measure clearly was intended to bolster material incentives since positive and negative bonuses were given for above or below average work. Underfulfillment carried a penalty of an equal percentage drop in wages; overfulfillment half the rate of increase above the norm. An upper ceiling was set, determined by the rule that total wages not surpass the minimum wage set for the next higher skill category. A progressive piece rate with no limits was thus shunned. This system of "salary scales with work norms" presumably implemented Lenin's dictum on distribution according to work; its piecework character is shown by this example of norm-setting:

> . . . if the norm set for plowing land with a tractor and plow of three discs in land of average quality is 50 square chains in a work-day of eight hours, and if this job is in Group V with a rate wage of 5.20 pesos, then the rate per square chain is found by dividing 5.20 by 50 . . . . That means the worker is paid at the rate of 10.4 centavos per square chain . . .[39]

Since the summer of 1967, a new wage policy more in accord with moral incentives was taken. The new principle was payment according to skills and hours worked, with wages unaffected by a rise or fall in production. Wage floors were gradually raised. There was a practical element in switching to time payments, a trend observed in other Communist countries. To begin with, there was often a tendency to revert to the simpler method of payment by time in many work centers. Norms were often incorrectly fixed; where they were found too high, they produced grumbling and when they were too low, "laxity in work discipline" resulted. Sometimes norm-setters would collude with workers and

39. Talavera and Herrera, "La organización del trabajo . . . ," p. 72.

managers in fixing them low. Then, too, norms were frequently readjusted in step with improved techniques and experience in production—which again caused grumbling. A laborer, expecting an upward revision of his norm, was tempted to cut down on his performance much like the enterprise manager in another context. And like the latter, the laborer was often induced by work quotas to maximize pieces with some neglect of quality. On the doctrinal side, the Ministry of Labor intimated a re-evaluation of the piecework system; payments for overtime would disappear first in order "to eliminate wage practices and scales which have become prejudicial to the complete development of communist consciousness." [40] The new wage policy seems to have been tried out first in industry; in agriculture it was later decided in the sugar industry "to base the amount of annual pay on the worker's highest qualification . . . it does not matter whether a pan operator works at some job calling for no special skill during the off season; that worker is a qualified pan operator, and his skill commands a specified pay . . ." [41]

The previous discussion suggests that the attempt to bolster material incentives in the mid-1960's was short-lived and was probably due to the inability of workers to realize their different money incomes in the consumer goods sector—aside from its cumbersomeness. We conclude that the wage differences that still exist today are of very limited allocative-incentive strength, and that for practical purposes, it can be said that the labor market is absent. This condition is the basic

40. Our source on this new labor policy is meager and confined mainly to the government paper, *Granma*. See its issues of September 8, 1968, p. 2 and October 27, 1968, p. 4. Our best journal sources were discontinued since late 1966 and the first half of 1967; the government has prohibited the exportation of the valuable *Gaceta Oficial*.

41. *Granma*, June 22, 1969, p. 4.

requirement for saying that Cuba (and China) relies primarily on the use of moral incentives over material ones; and another way of abolishing the labor market was by an equalitarian physical distribution of consumer goods.

No one dominating principle of wage formation emerges from our study of the new scales and work norms of the mid-1960's. There were several aims that wage policy was meant to achieve. Certainly greater equality was one; another, the formation of skills; still another was the purely accounting function of wages to facilitate the checking of a worker's technical efficiency over time. Yet one suspects the influence of the Marxian theory of value in the disregard for supply and demand factors in setting wages. The labor value theory made its influence known in the overly technocratic definition given to a phrase one often heard at this time, namely, "equal pay for the same work." The "same work" meant jobs requiring the same technological preparation; thus considerations of value in use and factor scarcity were neglected. A mathematical planning rule for deploying labor to its most valuable uses is "equal pay for work of the same value," where the relevant value is measured by the last worker's output. But this rule, which a live labor market would show a tendency in approximating, would have produced intolerable income effects (inequalities), and it went against the labor theory's bias for wages based on average occupational performance. This shows in Guevara's declaration (endorsed by Castro), namely, that "it is not right at the present time for two laborers, one in mining and another in the beer industry, to earn different salaries because the latter is more profitable, ignoring the fact that the two are socialist property." [42] Another related example is a typical denunciation of "some farmers [who] offered very high salaries to attract workers

42. Guevara, "Tareas industriales . . . ," *Cuba Socialista*, March, 1962, p. 43.

from other jobs—the phenomenon known as piracy of the labor force . . ."[43] The seeming simplicity of the new wage scales was contrasted by the leaders to the alleged anarchy of some 25,000 classifications and 90,000 different types of wages they inherited from market capitalism.[44] It can be shown, however, that this great number of wages and classifications may have a rationale in a market system. The argument is based on the principle of equal pay for work of equal value; since many individuals, particularly the highly skilled, are unique factors one would expect similarly unique salaries from the market.

Has Moral Stimulation Been A Success?

This question depends on whose goals we consider—choice criteria in regard to which success is said to have been achieved.[45] One goal was surely the replacement of the market in labor allocation and it is clear that the central administrators succeeded in this. In this connection, the main objective of the labor managers was a sheer increase in the volume of labor supplied and its redistribution in favor of agriculture. A scholarly attempt at measuring the value of what he calls "unpaid labor" has been made by Mesa-Lago. His findings show not only an increased volume of man-hours supplied in 1962 as compared to 1958 but a sustained increase in the value of national savings due to unpaid or voluntary labor from 1962 to 1967; "the annual average saving was more than

43. A. Martínez Sanchez, "Las normas de trabajo y escala salarial," *Nuestra Industria*, October, 1964, p. 43; also Talavera and Herrera, "La organización del trabajo . . ." p. 68.

44. J. R. Herrera and A. González, "Normas y escala salarial en la agricultura," *Cuba Socialista*, March, 1966, p. 61.

45. James O'Connor's comment that "social emulation was at least a partial failure . . ." from 1961 to 1963, is vague since he doesn't specify a success criterion. See his "The Organized Working Class . . . ," pp. 25–26.

$50 million, 1.4 percent of the yearly average of Cuba's national income during this period. . . ." He concludes that approximately 200,000 to 300,000 man-years were provided in 1967, or from 8 to 12 percent of the regular labor force, although a much larger number of individuals was involved." [46]

In terms of the number of individuals involved in volunteer work, its sustained growth seems indicative of success in pursuing another objective: the instilling of the work ethic of responding to moral incentives. An official count on April 2, 1967, showed some 75,000 volunteers for the Girón Fortnight, a work campaign commemorating the Bay of Pigs invasion. During the entire month of Girón, 250,000 were reported to have volunteered six days per week for either two, three, or four weeks.[47] Also, in other areas, another 150,000 volunteers took off for the rugged Escambray mountains to plant coffee while the massive agricultural development around Havana—its "Green Belt" program—in early 1967 drew mostly volunteers from the metropolitan area. The not entirely voluntary "School to the Countryside" program recruited 150,000 "volunteers" for the required six-week stint.[48] By late 1969, there were well over half of the programmed 100,000 "volunteers" in the Youth Centennial Column. The following facts were widely publicized in 1968 and were typical: 240,000 renounced payment for overtime work; 25,350 men turned their jobs over to women in order to join agricultural brigades; 3448 switched from the city to the country for two years and thousands upon thousands as-

46. C. Mesa-Lago, "Economic Significance of Unpaid Labor in Socialist Cuba," Reprinted from *Industrial and Labor Relations Review,* (Cornell University) April, 1969, pp. 350, 354.

47. *Granma,* April 9, 1967, p. 3; May 12, 1967, p. 3. A field observer, M. Frayn notes: "The standard work week in Cuba is 48 hours, but large numbers of workers volunteer to do unpaid overtime, sometimes another two hours a day, in certain circumstances as much as four." *The Globe and Mail* (Toronto), January 14, 1969.

48. *Granma,* October 1, 1967, p. 1; February 12, 1967, p. 4.

pired for Heroes of Moncada Banners, and so on.[49] In May of that year, workers in hotels and restaurants were persuaded by the government to renounce tipping on the grounds that the practice was "immoral."[50] The Deputy Prime Minister who is also Minister of the Army gave the following numbers in regard to recent successes with voluntary labor:

> Ninety-three thousand people were mobilized on a voluntary basis for 30 days to work in agricultural production, while the factories and workshops were manned by the same workers who will keep industry going in wartime. Both these groups of workers were organized into civil defense squads, platoons, companies, and battalions . . . . In the entire country a total of a quarter of a million volunteers were mobilized for two or three weeks or even the entire month.[51]

Note the trend in what Paul Sweezy and Leo Huberman have called "semi-militarization" and "regimentation."[52] Indeed, in the same speech, the Deputy Prime Minister praised the civil defense type of discipline and organization and announced its use for 1969–70 thus marking at least a short-term trend in its use. With the acceleration of investment in late 1966, reinforced by a cultural revolution just as profound as the one in China, moral incentives as well as administrative nonmarket means of recruiting labor may continue to be used through the decade starting in 1970, the anticipated period of take-off into self-sustaining rapid growth.

In late 1968 some 170,061 workers at 1348 work centers graded themselves from the category of "clockwatchers" to that of "communist workers" by renouncing overtime payments. As partial reward, social security of 100 percent of wages were extended to them.[53] Memberships to the advance-

---

49. *Granma*, June 30, 1968, pp. 4–5.
50. *Granma*, June 2, 1968, p. 8.
51. *Granma*, May 12, 1968, p. 3.
52. L. Huberman and P. Sweezy, *Socialism in Cuba*, Chapter 8.
53. *Granma*, December 15, 1968, p. 4.

guard movement are another indicator of the instilling of the new work ethic since only those who had proved themselves possessors of the communist work attitude were elected members. In mid-1968, there were some 120,107 known members. In the next year, membership jumped to nearly twice that number.[54] The elimination of most taxes by late 1969 suggests a greater internal motivation to work much more now for the community's or state's profits than for the sake of one's private material advantage. A related measure of the extent to which the new work mechanism has been internalized by workers and managers is the progressive elimination of all taxes in Cuba, and to a lesser extent, in China. By 1970, they had been virtually eliminated in the former. The cynic may claim that taxes have been merely hidden by paying workers much less than the value of their products rendered to state employers. But the transfer of income to the community by means of that mechanism indicates, it seems, greater willingness on the worker's part to contribute resources to the state. By not requiring the state to pay the value of their respective products as a pre-condition for working (which are then forcibly taxed later), both workers and managers display a form of selfless behavior. For 1970, Castro cited that 135 million hours were spent in the sugar harvest, equivalent to about 500,000 man-years of 260 days working for eight hours a day.[55] The number of nonmonetary award winners continued to increase. These data do not demonstrate voluntary decentralist behavior on the part of award winners, but it seems to suggest the formation of a significant vanguard among a work force of about 1,850,000 who respond to nonpecuniary benefits as symbolized by the receipt of various nonmonetary awards.

54. See *Granma*, June 30, 1968, pp. 4–5 and May 25, 1969, p. 4.
55. His August 23 Speech in *Granma*, August 30, 1970, p. 3.

CHAPTER FOUR

Efficiency and Growth
Under Moral Incentives

The crude figures cited in the previous discussion and Mesa-Lago's physical and value estimates of the cost-savings contribution of those workers recruited by use of moral incentives, show success in terms of the latter's ability to raise the volume of manhours worked and to raise the number of workers in the total population. Alternatively, previous studies of the system of moral incentives and the politico-administrative allocation of labor show success in terms of the former's ability to substitute for the labor market based on material incentives—in the specific Cuban context. But we are also interested in evaluating its success in terms of another criterion—its actual contribution to the sum total of useful material products (GNP). In the previous criterion we were not interested in evaluation in terms of an ultimate material purpose. Neither were we interested in evaluation in terms of the nonmaterial criterion of equity. In now turning to these questions we might define efficiency, both in its partial and global senses, as being concerned with the abilities of a productive organization in producing the greatest surplus of material benefits over input costs. The question of overall goodness, on the other hand, broadens the narrow concept of GNP by asking the question of growth of what for whom,

80

and by adding other social indicators, some of which are non-material. Recall that one main goal of moral stimulation is egalitarianism under which was subsumed the subgoal of full employment for its own sake. An evaluation of overall goodness would have to consider performance in terms of that social indicator as well as others, such as the level of education and health.

Success in Terms of GNP

In the following discussion, the question of material efficiency will be dealt with since by all accounts it is the chief social indicator of success in most people's minds, including those of the Cuban leaders. Also, the last main division of our investigation of moral incentives inquires into the historical stability of the system and, surely, one crucial pre-condition for its systemic survival is the ability of moral incentives to supply people with a rising level of ultimate material goods. In previous works dealing with moral stimulation in the labor sphere, no attempts have been made to assess the possible material losses, if any, associated with the micro-inefficiencies of nonmarket labor distribution, with the GNP gains associated with successes in raising the sheer volume of man-hours worked. In discussing this question of the nonmarket system's overall material efficiency, we can no longer abstract from the possibility that the greater supply from those committed to the present system may also have been diluted in terms of GNP lost by emigration from those dissatisfied with it. In discussing these intriguing questions, the reader should be warned that given the poor quality of the available data, and in many cases its virtual absence, our task seems to be an almost impossible one. Moreover, there is no statistical way of separating the different effects of various important causes that acted simultaneously on the behavior of efficiency and growth; these acted all at once and interactions among them were present. My justification in moving on just the same, in spite of these difficulties, is the absence of a superior alternative procedure; in addition, the crude procedure offered here yields fruitful and verifiable hypotheses.

Efficiency of the Communistic Rule

The previous chapter argued that the allocative mechanism of moral incentives so far seems workable and it was viewed as a technique within the administrative framework for its partial decentralization. Ideally, acting on the basis of moral incentives consisted in placing greater importance in enhancing community profits rather than one's own goals, including material ones. We assumed moral action to be something which a social group defines as "good" and for which reinforcements and sanctions are instituted. As Cuban socialism—now communism—enters its second decade, the planner-socializers (in China, too) have achieved a minimum amount of socialization of a wide segment of the population who by now seem to internally conform to the new cultural rules of behavior prescribed by the communist ethic, and which they think is implemented by the system of moral prizes. A great deal of social imitation of prize-winning exemplary models of socialist altruism and work has been produced. And in so far as moral stimulation works, it blunts the authoritarian bias of the administrative allocation of labor—in Cuba by the Labor Ministry's Regional Office and by other ministerial and administrative agencies. What might convince the skeptic about its preservation in the next decade at least, is the Cuban and Chinese leaders' awesome religious commitment to the communist allocative rule of "from each his ability, to each his need." This commitment seems to suggest other than material motives for resorting to moral incentives. The Cubans and Chinese claim that only under the unique set of institutions of prizes and the emulation of productive models can an egalitarian distribution be made compatible with increases in labor and managerial incentives to produce more. They imply, too, that production systems are classifiable on the basis of the primary role given to moral over private material incentives. Thus, the Soviet Union today is indistinguishable from the United States—on this basis. In the near period, the forces making for the adoption of an alternative morality based on market-private maximization of opportunities lie submerged underneath a heavy overlay of ideology.

My main interest here, however, is to formalize the operation of the allocative mechanism of moral incentives, to deduce its main efficiency characteristics, and to relate these to the Lewis-Fei-Ranis discussion of the possibility of taking-off by absorbing disguised unemployment. That discussion was limited to semi-feudal market economies, but, to quote Benjamin Higgins, "the truth is that redundant labor of the kind assumed by the authors [Fei and Ranis] is probably non-existent." [1] The reason, in Hla Myint's words, is that "the amount of 'disguised unemployment' depends on what we consider to be a full day's work for each." [2] Due to the income —and work-sharing devices of traditional economies, it is widely admitted that increased real wages in terms of incentive consumer goods would have to be paid to elicit more hours of work from those who remain in the old places of employment. Thus Higgin's plea that the term 'disguised unemployment' be eradicated enjoys wide acceptance. These objections are well taken but apply only to societies which envision a take-off within a market set of institutions.

I shall shortly illustrate the workings of the decentralist aspect of the Cuban and Chinese non-market mode of labor allocation—moral stimulation—by means of a graph. Like

1. Benjamin Higgins, *Economic Development* (New York: Norton, 1968), p. 320.
2. Hla Myint, *The Economics of Developing Countries* (New York: Praeger, 1965), p. 87.

the familiar market supply and demand curves for labor, the supply of manhours under moral incentives depends on decentralized behavior on our agent's part. The workers' response to the call to work more for the community than for themselves as manifested in the competition for prizes does not mean that workers respond to prizes only; they respond to administrative pressure too, as recently exemplified in Cuba by the calling of the civilian reserve to join the army for the 1970 sugar harvest.[3] And they also respond to the severely limited scale of wage differentials which are used as complementary material incentives. But the seemingly substantial monetary wage differences are illusory. Salaries have little relation to types of jobs since a typical 250 pesos-a-month industrial manager is, in terms of real consumables, closer to a 300 pesos-a-month skilled worker and a 95 pesos-a-month unskilled worker than one would otherwise think (due to consumer rationing and a commitment to provide large amounts of "free" services). Wages, as one of its main functions, operates as "passive accounting" thereby easing the checking and comparison of a worker's technical efficiency between different periods of time. For this purpose wages are fixed for relatively long periods, and the small wage differences were designed to encourage the long-run formation of technical skills. But they do not primarily allocate workers to their current uses nor are they designed to act as the main incentives in given places.

As an incidental but interesting comparison, our discussion of wages and moral incentives applies to China particularly after its Great Proletarian Cultural Revolution in 1966 which swept back the "economism" of the 1961–65 revisionist period. As in Cuba, the labor market with its highly variable wage differentials is not the main current allocator of laborers and managers to the labor market's various uses. This social task is carried out by administrative authorities and resort to comprehensive moral incentives. Wage

3. *Granma*, November 16, 1969, p. 3.

differentials have been narrowed; the bonus system has been abolished; and a return to time payments ushered in. Heavy use is made of a variety of exemplary models for emulation and a rich array of formal and informal titles arranged in a hierarchic order of official and social recognition. Enterprises, ministries, and other associations sponsor emulation contests and award several grades of prizes.[4] A Cuban counterpart might be a contest between one ministry's long-term voluntary women's brigade against another such brigade; and there are continued "meetings in work centers to discuss the work program in connection with the Heroic Guerrilla Award." And in the same flexible and *ad hoc* way, it might be a "special emulation organized in mechanized loading and transportation of cane in view of its importance in 1970 . . ."[5] Charles Hoffman writes of the Chinese system of moral incentives, which he regards as being essentially of a decentralist nature and as it functioned with less force before China's cultural revolution, as follows:[6]

> "Advanced" or "outstanding" workers are those who surpass certain standards of performance. "Models" are higher on the scale; they excel over time and are named from the best advanced workers. "Labor heroes" are at the pinnacle . . . , Special mention go to those who learn correctly from the models' examples.
>
> . . . .
>
> The crowning achievement for some workers is to be sent as representatives to the periodic conferences, regional and national, held to extol elite workers . . .

4. Charles Hoffman, *Work Incentive Practices and Policies in the People's Republic of China, 1953–1965* (New York: State University of New York Press, 1967), pp. 18, 19; pp. 64–65.
5. *Granma*, March 8, 1970, p. 4; August 17, 1969, pp. 1–3 respectively.
6. Hoffman, *Work Incentive* . . . , pp. 63–65. His book lists a comprehensive bibliography on the subject most of which I found at the Center for Chinese Studies in Berkeley.

The diagram below represents the cumulative effects of the institutionalization of different prizes on the supply of labor. At any given time, we can arrange the different kinds of prizes in a hierarchy of increasing ordinal importance as represented here by our vertical scale. By prize I shall mean all kinds of nonmonetary awards—be they mere intangible honorable mentions or tangible awards such as plaques, medals and paper certificates of merit. I shall not discuss the complex process of how a prize is institutionalized, although the last chapter touched on it. The degree of social importance of a

Shift Effect of Prizes on the Supply of Labor

Hierarchy of Prizes

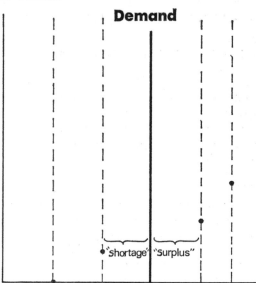

Supply of Labor in Manhours

INV.NO.
L.C.NO.

KXISA   06/14/72

UNIVERSITY OF ALABAMA PRESS

B4-289683
76-148691

THE THEORY OF MORAL INCENTIVES IN CUBA,
BY ROBERT M. BERNARDO. INTROD. BY IRVING
BERNARDO, ROBERT M.
UNIVERSITY, UNIVERSITY OF ALABAMA PRESS
X 159 P. 22 CM.

75/44

BOOK NO.

RD ABEL & CO.

FOR
ADDRESS

SELLING
PRICE

BACK

COPY 3

INVOICES

A = Richard Abel & Co., Nederland N.V., Van Hallstraat 167, Amsterdam, The Netherlands

B = 47 Athletic Field Rd., Waltham, Mass. 02154

C = 1312 27th Street, Zion, Illinois 60099

D = P. O. Box 10007, Denver, Colorado 80210

E = Richard Abel & Co. (England) Ltd., 6A Mill Trade Estate, Acton Lane, London N.W. 10, England

F = Richard Abel & Co., AG, Fischerweg 9, 3002 Berne, Switzerland

H = P. O. Box 241, Marion, Ohio 43302

J = P. O. Box 15469, Atlanta, Georgia 30302

K = Richard Abel & Co., Pty. Ltd. 1/33 Warraba Road, Narrabeen North, N.S.W. 2101 Australia

L = 1506 Gardena St., Glendale, California 91204

N = 1001 Fries Mill Rd., Blackwood, New Jersey 08012

P = P. O. Box 4245, Portland, Oregon 97208

S = Industrial Center Bldg., Gate 5 Road, Marinship, Sausalito, California 94965

T = Richard Abel & Co. (Canada) Ltd., 128 Industrial Rd., Richmond Hill, Ontario, Canada

X = 3434 Dalworth St., Arlington, Texas 76010

prize depends on the difficulty of earning it, on the scarcity of the number of identical prizes of that particular kind or category, for example on the number of Heroes of Labor awards in contrast to the number of advance guard awards. And the ordinal rank of a particular kind of prize also depends on the sum of social honors associated with the particular kind of prize. But the value-rank of a prize is probably chiefly determined by its scarcity—the Hero of Moncada Banner in Cuba, for example, is more highly rated than an advance-guard title; by end of 1969, six percent of the working population had won it whereas there were many more winners of the advance guard title by that date. Thus, also, the Hero of Labor both in Cuba and China, is clearly the most prestigious and would occupy the highest category in our vertical scale. The sum of honors attaching to it, the difficulty of acquiring it, and its limitation in number to several dozens a year make it the highest title to which one may aspire. Election into the Party belongs to a lower category but it ranks higher than election into the advance-guard (vanguard) movement since the latter is easier to obtain and the number of prizes in that category are numerous. Workers are kept well informed of the various categories of moral titles or banners through the various official publicity organs, the Party, the neighborhood committees, and the manpower administration as a whole. Every citizen is daily urged to show a communitarian spirit by competing for these prizes and, in so far as the total manhours of labor supplied vary also with offers of titles, our diagram shows the cumulative "advertising" effect of prizes on the supply of labor. This is shown by the shift of the supply of labor as each prize is institutionalized; each vertically dotted line showing the particular supply of labor corresponding to each kind of prize. The diagram above shows that prizes can be regarded as the money of moral incentives with the important exception that the former cannot be spent on material goods including the hiring of people's services. Thus Cuban and

Maoist thought regard it as a practicable means of implementing not only "to each his need" but also "from each his ability." And it is also a way of tapping competitive and status urges in a socially approved manner. From this comparative point of view, it is instructive to deduce the efficiency characteristics of our moral response curve brought about by the shift in the supply of labor. Note that the relative value of a set of identical prizes, called prize here, is given by a ranking scale which changes in discrete jumps according to the changing nature or quality of the prize. This results in the difficulty of finely tuning the system of labor deployment, as would otherwise be possible under a system of finely graduated money wages. We would thus expect, on *a priori* grounds, that a new prize-category introduced to elicit manhours may sometimes "undershoot" the required predetermined amount of labor, but it could "overshoot" the mark as well. These *a priori* events have, in fact, been reported by the Labor Minister himself when he noted occasional surpluses of workers in one place in the presence of deficits elsewhere.[7]

The number of surplus man-hours probably exceeds the number of deficits in given places. This is due to the lack of a strict constraint on the prizes a ministry, firm, or the organizing committee of a work project may obtain for distribution or grant on its own. True, authorities in the planning and manpower administration, particularly the latter's agency in charge of socialist emulation, who have control over the issues of titles, have publicly advised against the debasement of a prize through prize-inflation. In practice, they have been permissive as witness the recent large numbers of advance-guard prizes issued in recent years. By expanding the number of identical prizes in a particular prize-set, the latter's rank and effectiveness are reduced. Moreover, prize-inflation occurs by instituting new sets of prizes. A plethora of new prizes have been introduced in connection with the many special

7. *Granma*, August 4, 1968, p. 4.

emulation drives and in connection with work drives on the occasion of a national historic date. Able to issue new prizes by either method just described, many organizers of work projects tended to waste labor because they lacked the discipline of a limited budget constraint. A way of improving the system of moral incentives would seem to lie in imposing strict limits on the issue of tangible and intangible titles for additional manhour supplies and in defining more strictly the process of their creation. For example, the number of advance guard awards at the workshop and brigade levels are not clearly delimited; and the Party, the labor organization, the ministries, and other campaign organizers either issue some new titles or are able to obtain such approval from the manpower administration.

Lacking a wage-costing system that might help approximate relative costs of work projects, administrators of the nonmarket system of labor allocation are not likely to adjust the worker's cost to the value of his contribution. Thus an observer reported recently that "labor costs for new projects were often scarcely estimated." [8] An employer operating in markets would have no incentive for employing additional manhours past the point where its contribution to the firm's revenue is zero or below the guaranteed institutional wages. Our nonmarket employer might on occasion unwittingly do so. In a labor-scarce setting, where the value of the products added by a worker exceeds the minimum wage, this leads to waste. In a labor surplus setting, it is not necessarily a sign of inefficiency since the institutional wage might well lie above the value contribution of the available supply of manhours. In countries with large overt unemployment and underemployed workers, the institutional wage is above the value productivity of a sizable number of workers. Allocation ac-

8. As reported by a planner and friend of Michael Frayn's; see his field report "Cuba Today" in *The Globe and Mail* (Toronto), January 14, 1969.

cording to the market criterion of hiring laborers only until wages equal the last man's net contribution to the revenues of the firm leads to wasteful unemployment. Under the system of moral incentives, employment of additional manhours or workers will likely continue even if the latter's current value of production is below the minimum guaranteed wage or even if its value is zero. For all the reasons just cited, full and overfull employment is the more likely situation under a system of moral incentives. True, overt full employment is achieved at the cost of substantial featherbedding; but this only means that the phase of totally absorbing a labor surplus, the so-called period of extensive development, has yet to be completed. In the meantime, an overt unemployment and visible underemployment rate which in the old days was one of the highest in Latin America was eliminated in Cuba by 1964.

The following diagram is adapted from the standard tool-kit associated with Professors Lewis, Fei, and Ranis.[9] It illustrates the comparative allocative characteristics just mentioned and suggests new ones. It is an oversimplified one-sector aggregative model but helpful.

The labor surplus under a market system is DF; it has been called disguised unemployment, but note that it may be visible to the observer's naked eye. The labor surplus is a market phenomenon which owes its existence to the failure of incentives among private producers for profit. A government planning agency anxious to maximize growth would seek to employ the barely productive and train redundant workers; but if it does so under the actual market constraint imposed by OW, the entire product would nearly be consumed by the total wages of a fully employed labor force, leaving no surplus that could be sold abroad for the estimated required capital

9. Gustav Ranis and John Fei, "A Theory of Economic Development," *American Economic Review*, Papers and Proceedings, September, 1961.

Macro-allocation in the Two Systems

Value of products and wages

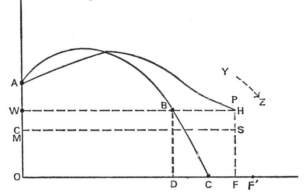

Laborers per period

Legend:
ABCF	=	Value of added products by laborers employed
WB	=	Supply of labor under market-material incentives
OW	=	Institutional market wage
WBH	=	Supply of labor under planned full employment via market-material incentives
AP	=	Value of the average product
DC	=	Barely productive labor
CF	=	Redundant labor, whose additions to GNP equal zero
OF	=	Full employment at a customary eight-hour day
OM	=	Biological survival wage
CS	=	Supply of labor under planned full employment via nonmarket moral incentives
OCSF	=	Total wage bill under moral incentives
CWHS	=	Marketable surplus abroad
FF'	=	Extra labor surplus due to increase in the customary working day (contributed or unpaid overtime). This extra labor surplus is measured in man-equivalents working eight hours a day that the extra unpaid hours are equivalent to.
YZ	=	potential added products of the extra labor surplus

inputs. Under a nonmaterial nonmarket system, real wages are reduced to accommodate the entire working population and leave enough surplus for the purchase of accompanying capital inputs and foreign technicians. Under the nonmarket system, DC or DF workers are overtly employed but their employment is really a disguised form of training for the sake of greater future outputs. At any rate, the lower real wages in the nonmarket system permit a high rate of savings which in the Cuban example has risen to nearly a third of national income in recent years.

There are several ways by which the real wage *per worker* is made to fall in spite of a constant or even rising money wage. This is accomplished by limited inflation of the total wage bill by issuing money as new workers are employed; by rationing of essential consumer goods; by reallocation of consumer goods into its public form such as communal dining, buses, communal housing, and so on. In terms of real wages per hour worked, a mechanism used to make it fall is the institutionalization of overtime voluntary work after regular hours and on weekends, a device which has raised the customary working day in Cuba probably by an average of two hours daily. The latter's addition to social product is large since it includes labor from all kinds of workers.

Let us now look at some empirical data to test our theory. The relative size of salaries in the various branches are roughly the same for Brazil, Chile, Colombia—and to a lesser extent, Venezuela. Cuba's alone are significantly out of line in being very high, reflecting in part presence of substantial underutilization of labor. These partial statistics, however, do not directly show relative efficiency. They are comparative data on average labor productivity in various branches in a selected number of countries and they need not indicate comparative inefficiency for Cuba. They point to inefficiency if we are willing to assume rough similarity in factor proportions between any two countries being compared and, in addition, we must assume that demand proportions for the groups of commodities in question are comparable across the countries being compared. These assumptions are not very unrealistic: factor proportions and demand structures, especially in the modern sector, seem roughly similar in the countries above. Furthermore, the figures suggest comparative industrial productivities of labor and the room for choosing alternative combinations among the factors of production in the modern "enclave" sector of a low income country is generally held to be small.

TABLE I

Share of Wages in Gross Industrial Value

Industrial Branches	Brazil 1960	Chile 1957	Colombia 1960	Venezuela 1961	Cuba 1964
Food, Beverages & Tobacco [a]	0.19	0.19	0.17	0.21	0.47
Textiles	0.35	0.31	0.31	0.43	0.60
Footwear & other Articles	0.37	0.33	0.37	0.41	0.55
Lumber and Furniture	0.32	0.30	0.46	0.57	0.98
Paper	0.22	0.28	0.24	0.34	0.46
Printing	0.36	0.41	0.42	0.48	0.55
Leather	0.29	0.34	0.28	0.36	0.40
Rubber	0.19	0.23	0.31	0.31	0.29
Chemicals	0.20	0.26	0.22	0.28	0.21
Petroleum Derivatives [b]		0.08	0.19	0.23	0.16
Non-metallic Minerals	0.28	0.33	0.35	0.36	0.61
Basic Metals	0.27	0.22	0.12	0.62	0.63
Machinery	0.28	0.36	0.41	0.43	0.67
Others	0.32	0.29	0.29	0.40	0.52
Average [c]	0.26	0.21	0.29	0.31	0.51

[a] Excludes the Sugar Industry
[b] Included in Chemicals
Source: JUCEPLAN, *Cuba Socialista*, May, 1966, p. 110. It cites these countries and the United Nations as other sources.
[c] My computation.

Thus, the data indicate comparative inefficiency. They, however, reflect well on the pursuit of egalitarianism—one of the principal objectives of moral stimulation. The data suggest the actual operation of the *a priori* micro-inefficiencies noted earlier. Note the inflation of the total money wage bill: to employ the visible labor, surplus new money was printed to a limited extent. Overfull employment is suggested; overt unpaid unemployment and underemployment disappeared at the cost of substantial *paid* hidden

TABLE II

Differences in Average Salaries Per Employed Person by Industries in Selected Latin American Countries

(Indices Refer to the Average of the Industry)

Industrial Branches	Brazil 1960	Chile 1957	Colom-bia 1960	Mexico 1960	Peru 1960	Vene-zuela 1961	Cuba 1964
Food, Beverages & Tobacco	82.3	101.8	98.2	84.9	85.5	91.9	97.0
Textiles	84.8	84.4	107.0	99.0	123.3	93.0	112.0
Footwear & Related Items	89.6	74.9	62.0	55.4	71.7	75.6	92.0
Lumber & Furniture	77.5	70.2	73.0	74.2	74.4	84.8	88.0
Paper	108.4	122.3	109.1	142.6	103.2	116.5	109.0
Printing	117.7	149.2	108.1	119.7	128.4	114.9	113.0
Leather	83.9	103.8	88.9	83.4	83.0	76.3	115.0
Rubber	140.5	114.6	129.1	141.9	184.1	127.5	122.0
Chemicals	138.4	130.5	132.9	150.8	110.5	136.0	108.0
Petroleum Derivatives [a]		168.4	320.5	161.3	85.4	212.6	187.0
Non-metallic Minerals	76.0	106.9	88.2	102.6	120.9	102.0	101.0
Basic Metals	123.2	161.5	125.3	150.9	120.9	129.7	111.0
Machinery	141.2	99.5	105.1	95.6	92.7	94.7	97.0
Others	108.3	79.7	95.7	89.6	88.6	69.4	92.0

[a] Included under chemicals.
Source: same as Table I.

unemployment much of it actually being training costs. The take-off through the complete absorption of the labor surplus has yet to be completed, for lack of sufficient accompanying capital tools and innovation. The micro-inefficiencies may, however, be over-compensated by macro gairs in GNP from increases in manhours due to the absorption of the labor surplus and donated overtime. Growth in GNP need not follow, as some have suggested, the Chinese example where the intensification of moral incentives was accompanied by attacks on technical experts, and where savings were allocated into low-yielding projects, as Castro candidly revealed in his July 26, 1970 speech. However, the elimination of a visible unemployment and underemployment rate which in 1958 were 10 and 6 percent was accomplished. Work hours have increased and so has the growth of donated labor equivalent to 12 percent of regular employment in 1967.[10]

Finally, a consideration of the efficiency of the mechanism of nonmonetary (moral) incentives must confront the expert work of the Economic Research Service of the United States Department of Agriculture. Its index of agricultural production seems to have been carefully constructed on the basis of data on Cuba's fourteen main agricultural products. These data, moreover, are not in dispute. These are its findings: [11]

	1957–59 (base)	1959	1960	1961	1962
Total Agriculture	100	104	99	101	80
	1963	1964	1965	1966	1967	1968 *
Total Agriculture	70	79	87	75	87	80

* Preliminary.

The index can be used as a springboard for tackling the

10. C. Mesa-Lago, "Economic Significance . . . ," p. 354.
11. See its *Indices of Agricultural Production for the Western Hemisphere*, March, 1969 (ERS-Foreign 264).

next question that has to be answered in evaluating the over-
all material efficiency of the nonmarket system of moral incentives in the allocation of additional supplies of manhours.
Were departures from optimal resource allocation overcom-
pensated by increases in the size of the gross national product?
In following my discussion of this topic, the reader should
bear in mind that we are also interested in the timing of certain
changes in GNP since it was not till about 1964, by many accounts, that the system of moral incentives was institutionalized into a workable arrangement. However, the previous
four years can be considered as an installation cost of the
system. In the long discussion which now follows, I shall
also touch on the loss to GNP due to the emigration of skilled
persons who were dissatisfied with the system. But for scientific reasons, a discussion of statistical bases is also included.

Note that the agricultural output index stood at 80 points
compared to the pre-socialist years of 1957–59, whose average
is given a value of 100 in the index. This figure is highly suggestive. Since agriculture contributes about 31 percent [12] of
national income and industrial policy after failing was reversed in mid-1963, to mention just one reason, it is hard to
see why national income in 1968 should be higher than in
1958. Indeed, Huberman and Sweezy, although they agree
with the contrary official view, hint darkly at an alternative
guess when they write that "it is now nearly 1969, and it is
clear that the envisaged goals are for most part not in sight.
. . . Cubans are still living on a severely austere diet. . . ." [13]

Because of its pivotal importance in the Cuban GNP
and in the various GNP estimators, a discussion of the sugar
statistics is enlightening. It was responsible for about 80 per-

12. This is based on the classic work by the International Bank
for Reconstruction and Development, *Report On Cuba* (Baltimore:
John Hopkins University Press, 1961), p. 35. The figure held in 1954
and may be slightly off in 1968.
13. Huberman and Sweezy, *Socialism in Cuba*, p. 200.

cent of the value of Cuba's exports, its share in national income varying from one-quarter to one-third. Its agricultural aspect accounted for 16 percent national income and its manufacturing and distributive aspects contributed 9 percent.[14] In regard to its relative share in total agricultural out-

TABLE III

Sugar Production

Year	Volume (In thousands of Metric Tons)
1957–1958 (Avg.)	5,729
1959	5,962
1960	5,804
1961	6,870
1962	4,815
1963	3,800
1964	3,800
1965	6,000
1966	4,500
1967	6,000
1968	5,231
1969	5,000
1970	8,512

Sources: Dudley Seers, *Cuba*, pp. 112, 131 (data up to 1962); for 1963, *Business Week*, September 14, 1963; for 1964, *Comercio Exterior*, December, 1964; for 1965, 1966 and 1967 (preliminary estimate), Economic Research Service, U.S. Department of Agriculture, *Western Hemisphere Agricultural Situation* (1967), p. 10. The 1967 estimate is confirmed by *Granma*, June 18, 1967, p. 1. The 1968 figure is from the Economic Research Service, *op. cit.*, its *1968 Midyear Review* of October, 1968, pp. 3–4; it blames the 1967–68 drought for this; its finding agrees entirely with the accounts in the Cuban press. For 1969, see *The Guardian*, (Cuba Supplement), July 25, 1969, p. 3; for 1970, *Granma*, July 26, 1970, p. 5.

14. *Investment in Cuba* (Washington, D.C.: U.S. Department of Commerce, 1957), p. 6.

put (at producers' prices, 1958), the sugar cane crop contributed 36.5 percent.[15]

The sugar output, in spite of its great importance, is not entirely reliable as a predictor of the relative movement of national income. A case in point is the remarkable sugar harvest of 1961; a one million ton increase in sugar over the previous year raised the agricultural index of the Economic Research Service of the United States Department of Agriculture by only two points. Curiosity surrounds the record sugar output of 1961. Dr. Pazos attributes the bumper crop to the fear among private sugar growers that unless they fully cultivated their cane lands, they would be taken over by the new government.[16] Pazos' view is plausible, since one of the provisions of the Agrarian Reform of May, 1959 was the compulsory cultivation of all privately owned latifundia and other large farms on pain of being subject to government expropriation. Data supplied by Andrés Bianchi is consistent with the view expressed above: in 1959, 77.6 percent of the available cane was harvested; in 1960 it rose to 83.1 percent. The harvested area was 98.2 percent in 1961.[17]

A related reason to the extensive sugar crop was the postponement of nationalization so as not to disrupt the 1960 harvest which ended in late May; it was in June and July of 1960 that nationalization began in earnest in agriculture. Being a kind of perennial grass, enjoying good weather and being harvested fully, the 1961 sugar crop proved to be one of the best in Cuba's history. The low sugar harvests of 1962 and 1963 were due to the policy of de-emphasizing sugar and, though re-emphasized again in mid-1963, an unusually bad series of tropical hurricanes and a long spell of intense

15. D. Seers, ed., *Cuba*, p. 341. He (Bianchi) cites INRA as his source.

16. Felipe Pazos, "Comentarios a dos artículos sobre la Revolución Cubana," *Trimestre Económico* (Mexico), January–March, 1962, pp. 6–7.

17. A. Bianchi in Seers, *Cuba*, pp. 112, 404, footnotes 31–2.

droughts are held responsible by all observers as the main causes of the low outputs of 1964, 1966, and 1968. The low sugar crop of the 1969 harvest of five million tons may have been partially affected by the drought as well as preparations for the ten-million sugar output of 1970.[18] However, that figure refers to the normal harvest period; we know that the harvest for 1970 was started some four months ahead in mid-July of 1968.

We now come to the central focus of this discussion— what is the relative size of national income eleven years later in comparison to 1958? The official position is that on the whole national income increased "modestly" in this period. This claim is, incidentally, supported by Wilbur F. Buck of the United States Department of Agriculture who writes that "Cuba's gross national product has risen from $2.7 billion in 1958 to nearly $3.0 billion in 1967. But per capita income has declined nearly 14 percent, to $368 . . ."[19]

Probable Path of GNP

I believe it is possible to infer the probable path of Cuban GNP in the past twelve years from the partial data now available. In the following discussion on statistical sources and their reliability, I refrain from getting too involved in details, nor do I attempt a comprehensive and thorough calculation of Cuban GNP since this is not the main focus of this book. I merely synthesize here what seems a reasonable if tentative hypothesis based on the best partial evidence we have.

Unfortunately, the Cuban government does not supply any outside agencies, including the United Nations, with national income data at constant prices. Those it releases are fragmentary, lack yearly continuity, and are vaguely specified

18. On the "normal" harvest of 1969, see *The Guardian* (Cuba Supplement), July 26, 1969, p. 3.

19. Wilbur F. Buck in *Foreign Agriculture*, January 6, 1969, p. 2, Vol. VII, No. 1, published by the U.S. Department of Agriculture.

as to the base-year of comparison and not always reliable. The regular publication of statistical yearbooks ceased in early 1960 and although systematic and comprehensive national income accounting seems to have been resumed in 1964, secrecy prevents researchers from obtaining the data. Official statistics on which previous views of Cuban national income were based were later rectified—for example, the United Nations Economic Commission for Latin America's (ECLA) Economic Survey of 1965 changed parts of the statistical tables on Cuba contained in its 1964 survey of Latin America.[20] The early official claims have been doubted by all serious investigators for this reason as well as others. There was a strong tendency in the early period to misreport data—perhaps unconsciously—by eager subordinates and enthusiasts heady with revolutionary euphoria. Also, statistics were released in part for their dramatic model effects. To the problem of secrecy we can add another: much of the data do not exist or are not comparable to the standard procedures of national income defined by the United Nations and accepted in non-Communist countries.[21]

20. A painstaking and detailed attempt at tracing the path of Cuban GNP is being attempted by Dr. Carmelo Mesa-Lago and will be published in his forthcoming book of original contributions, *Revolutionary Change in Cuba: Polity, Economy, Society*. It is based on the latest sources and developed in his Cuba seminar group at the University of Pittsburgh. A valuable survey, bibliography, and evaluation of Cuban statistical sources will be found in his "Availability and Reliability of Statistics in Socialist Cuba," *Latin American Research Review*, Spring, 1969.

21. An alternative basis from which to start in constructing the path of Cuban GNP is the *Boletín Estadístico de Cuba, 1962–1966* which should be published by UCLA in late 1970 or early 1971. Also, another official source, *Compendio Estadístico de Cuba* (issues from 1965 to 1968) is available, for instance, at the Center for Latin American Studies at Berkeley.

The *Boletín* shows a gross national product of slightly over three billion pesos in 1962 which increased by nearly a billion in 1966. In

Let us recall from the works of others that there was statistical neglect from late 1959 through 1961 and quality as a whole continued to suffer through 1963. In May, 1967 Cuba's delegation to the Twelfth Conference of ECLA [22] released only partial data on the more favorable components of national income and a recent field observer's vain efforts to penetrate the Central Planning Board for the kind of data we require confirms Dudley Seers and his associates' similar experience in 1962, as they relate in their book cited in this discussion. Sweezy and Huberman's recent work, although directed towards the issue of national income a decade later, does not offer new evidence on this issue and merely gives us the official claim that over-all material achievement in production (national income) in the past decade was "modest." [23]

A reminder needs to be made in interpreting national income data in a nonmarket setting. In a market society, the pressures of competition and the firm's ability to substitute inputs in the production process allows consumers and suppliers to adjust prices to some kind of approximation of relative desirabilities. Thus, national income is a crude indicator of material welfare. In Cuba the prices used in aggregating national income components do not measure relative desirabilities and costs; but there is another reason for not unduly using Cuban national income estimates as indicators of wel-

relation to GNP in 1959, the 1962 figure is significantly higher but means little since we don't know how much of the latter is due to inflation, or to a change in concepts of national income which neglects services. In addition, their procedures are not explained, in contrast to the U.S. Department of Agriculture studies cited here.

22. See, respectively, *Comercio Exterior* (Mexico), June, 1967, pp. 471–73; M. Frayn, *The Globe and Mail* (Toronto), January 14, 1969.

23. Huberman and Sweezy, *Socialism in Cuba*. Note the contrast with their late 1960 (after the embargo) prediction that "in perhaps five to ten years the Cuban national income could be doubled. . . ." *Cuba: Anatomy Of A Revolution* (New York: Monthly Review, 1961), p. 202.

fare since its redistribution may just be as important. In this regard, Cuban achievements in income leveling and in favor of public health and education are noteworthy. The national income estimates cited here are best regarded, in view of the foregoing argument, as measures of the changes in the over-all productive activity and capability of Cuban society to muster resources in producing a given list of outputs. And since in both systems the most useful information that national income statistics give us is the time-rate of change in productive activity (and changes in the stock of capital) we shall not be too concerned with the accuracy of actual levels.

The Main Views on Cuban National Income

None of our many views on Cuban national income (GNP) since 1960 to the present time, are authoritative due to the lack of sufficient data needed for such a calculation. National income estimates of the past eleven years or so are guesses at its most likely path. Yet some guesses are more informed than others and it is in this exploratory spirit in which I shall offer a view of the probable movement of Cuban national income since 1960. Let us first deal, however, with the official views.

The official accounts of the early years are discredited by the lack of statistics, indeed by its near abandonment during the early years of Cuban socialism. The official accounts are also characterized by vagueness. For example, national income is given in current prices without taking into account the effect of the appreciable inflation since 1960; and occasionally base-years are not well-defined in the official estimates of yearly growth rates. And some of the official accounts even contradict each other. For example, leading planners of the early period such as Juan Noyola and Regino Boti gave a growth rate of 10.5 and 12.3 percent respectively for 1960 relative to 1959.[24] Osvaldo Dorticós cited a yearly average growth rate of nearly 7 percent from 1958 to 1962;[25] but JUCEPLAN much later admitted that there was "stagnation in per capita product' from 1961 to 1963 although "important increases in per capita produc:" were enjoyed in 1964–65.[26] Castro's admission of a drop in production in "the first few years"[27] is in line with JUCEPLAN's and might serve as a starting point in tracing the relative ordinal path of national income, as measured, let us say, in 1953 Cuban relative prices. The decline did not occur in 1959 since, by all accounts, this was a very good year for national income. Dr. Felipe Pazos estimated a 5 to 6 percent growth rate over 1958 on the basis of national income statistics still collected by the National Bank of Cuba, which he then headed and the agency in charge of such computations until early 1960.[28] We know, as the data cited shows, that agricultural production in 1959, 1960, and 1961 was comparable with previous years. The drop in production referred to by Castro must refer to either 1960 or 1961 and is attributable chiefly to a large negative change in industrial or non-agricultural production. I shall advance an argument for dating the drop in over-all production as of 1960. However, before we proceed, let us note a celebrated

24. See Juan Noyola, "La revolución cubana y sus efectos en el desarrollo económico," *El Trimestre Económico*, Vol. 28 (3), (July–September, 1961), p. 418 and Regino Boti, "El Plan de la economía nacional para 1963," *Cuba Socialista*, April, 1963, p. 24; his article in the same journal, December, 1961, p. 28.

25. Osvaldo Dorticós, *Cuba Socialista*, January, 1963, p. 7.

26. JUCEPLAN, "El desarrollo industrial de Cuba," *Cuba Socialista*, April, 1966, pp. 50–51.

27. The reference is to his "At the time when our production was dropping during the first few years, [Soviet aid was essential] . . . in *Granma*, January 5, 1969, p. 6.

28. Felipe Pazos, "Comentarios a dos artículos sobre la Revolución Cubana," *Trimestre Económico*, January–March 1962, pp. 6–10.

early attempt at "estimating" the relative movement of Cuban GNP from 1959 to 1965.

> Although the gross national product may have increased by as much as 3 to 5 per cent in 1965 due mainly to the recovery in sugar production, it failed to recover much of the more than 15 per cent decline of the previous 6 years and resulted in a per capita output of $365—only about 85 per cent of the 1958 level.[29]

Wilbur F. Buck of the Economic Research Service has kindly described their general procedures to me, as well as the source of the 15 percent figure.

> The estimated 15 percent decline in the Cuban economy from 1958, as noted in ERS-Foreign 154, was based on a release by the United States Department of State in 1966. The estimated 3 to 5 percent growth of Cuban gross national product for 1965 to which you refer was developed through evaluating the information gathered from a number of sources. This included our knowledge and experience within this area, particularly our familiarity with the Cuban agricultural plant and its capabilities; data appearing in trade journals; foreign country trade statistics; Cuban broadcasts; weather records for the area; and accounts given by refugees and foreign visitors to Cuba. Considerable information is generally available with regard to Cuba, but most of it is fragmentary and its sources and purposes require careful consideration.
>
> Agricultural indices were developed in a manner similar to that used for computing the GNP. Generally, we feel that the indices of agricultural output are reasonably accurate as indicators due to the heavy weight of sugar on which we have reasonably good information and to reports on agricultural growing conditions, consumption and trade relating to other commodities.[30]

29. Economic Research Service, U.S. Department of Agriculture, *The Western Hemisphere Agricultural Situation* (Washington, D.C., March, 1966) (ERS–Foreign 154), p. 21.

30. From his May 17, 1967 letter to me.

I have not been able to obtain a copy of the U.S. Department of State release—it does not seem to be accessible.[31] At any rate, State Department releases seldom mentioned methodology and one would probably not find the nature of its 15 percent estimate explained there. Even so, it seems clear who the State Department's source was. In *Castroism, Theory and Practice*, Draper wrote:

> . . . Minister of Economy Regino Boti calculated that the rate of growth of the Cuban economy for 1962–1965 would be between 10 and 14 percent annually (a far cry from its decline by 15–20 percent).

Draper based his estimate on René Dumont's *Cuba: Socialisme et Développement*, whom he quotes on the same page:

> Dumont concludes: 'After progressing in 1959–60, due above all to better distribution (of resources), the level of Cuban life stagnated in 1961; and it fell perhaps 15 to 20 per cent in 1962, with strict rationing.'

Dumont, in turn intuited his 15 percent estimate from his first-hand experience of Cuba.

Loss Due to Emigration

I shall argue that the decline in Cuban national income began sometime in 1960—the first year of the comprehensive administrative socialist experiment. My argument is that during this year a massive brain drain of immense proportions occurred. But not only was this previous accumulation of human talent depleted but so were other stocks of wealth such as livestock and inventories. If we consider the loss of services due to these drains on capital stock and subtract them from the gross data on national income, the loss to

31. I did not find it in the U.S. Department of State [Releases] For the Press for 1966.

Cuban national income is quite staggering. Ideally, national income is computed by summing up all yearly sums of services and consumption enjoyed or received by a group of individuals (the nation) during a period of time without depleting capital stocks. We ought to capitalize the present and discounted future costs due to the depletion of the stock of technical skills. The definition above and the discounting procedure suggested are methodologically unwieldy in practice. Let us adopt a compromise which is close to the actual procedures used. Let us define GNP as the sum of gross investment and consumption where net investment includes inventories. Furthermore, let us treat all forms of capital as capable of being varied; in our definition, net investment may assume large negative values.

MacGaffey and Barnett conducted a survey which suggests the magnitude of the loss due to the severe depletion of human talent incurred that year. As of December, 1960 their survey showed 69 percent of the thirty thousand or more refugees in Miami were either white collar workers or professional people.[32] Richard Jolly's research puts an estimate of between fifteen and twenty thousand technicians and/or professionals in the group of a quarter million who had left Cuba by the end of 1962.[33] He found that the total number of this class was between eighty-six thousand and one hundred thousand.[34] Moreover, most of those who left did so in the second half of 1959 and throughout 1960. Let us assume that national income for 1958 was 2,210 million pesos, and that real income increased by 6 percent in 1959. Again, let us

32. Wyatt MacGaffey and Clifford R. Barnett, *Cuba, Its People, Its Society, Its Culture* (New Haven: Human Relations Area Press, 1962), p. 273.
33. Richard Jolly in D. Seers, *Cuba*, p. 177.
34. Ibid., pp. 177, 415. This class does not include managers, administrators, who numbered 94,000, nor does it include skilled laborers.

assume another fact: that the average technician and professional (in Miami by December 1960) used to receive an average salary of $500 a month, a reasonable figure under Cuban
conditions. Then the loss of output due to this source alone
(20,700 men) yields a number of about 5 percent of GNP for
1959. Here, we are making some "heroic" assumptions but
this is somewhat offset by other considerations we shall mention. The assumption is that there was full employment of
managers and technicians and that the thirty-thousand or so
who left from mid-1959 to December, 1960 had all left by
January 1, 1960. We also ignored the direct and indirect
losses which were avoided by substitutions and relocations of
other inputs such as foreign technicians and managers and
Cubans who were quickly trained to replace the exiles. However, the one-to-six-months, large-scale manpower training
programs called *Mínimo Técnico*, were not started until the
second trimester of 1962.[35] And university reform in the
direction of scientific and technical education began even
later—in 1963.[36] The inflow of skilled persons and other forms
of capital from Eastern Europe, Latin America and other
countries, helped to prevent a collapse in the management and
operation of productive units. But they were imperfect substitutes; our authority here is René Dumont who, in his
September, 1963 report to the Cuban government, observed
that "Foreign contribution, in capital and technicians, in spite
of being plentiful, has not been sufficient to assure a satisfactory agricultural development." [37] The losses incurred in sub-

35. M. Nolff in D. Seers, ed., *Cuba*, p. 308.
36. In 1962, René Dumont states ". . . 22 degrees in agronomy
were granted (one third of those before the [civil] war)." He suggests
that this was typical in 1962 and 1963. See his *Cuba: Intento de crítica
constructiva* (Barcelona: Editorial Nova Terra, 1965), p. 154. This
book is a Spanish translation of his *Cuba, Socialisme et Développement*.
37. His report is partially reproduced in Cuban Economic Research Project, *Cuba, Agriculture and Planning*, pp. 248–50.

sequent years due to the depletion of human capital in 1960 are difficult to measure. Let us abstract from this problem and the discounting procedure associated with it. We do not customarily include human capital in national accounts which, when added to consumption, shows a decline in GNP. We can, therefore, think of it in terms of the skilled persons lost, multiplied by their productivity (which we crudely measured in terms of their average wage). Counting the products lost in 1960 this way, we get a rough estimate of a 5 percent decline in GNP for 1960 in relation to 1959. We can apply the same procedure to other capital stock which declined in 1960, but simply mention it to suggest the conservativeness of the above estimate of the decline in GNP. There was evidence of decline in other capital assets. Dorticós acknowledged the neglect of replacement investment during the early years of the new system.[38] Inventories declined in 1960; and the animal stock, cattle particularly, declined that year.[39]

Other Data on Non-agricultural Output:
Tobacco, Cement, Transport

Because tobacco was Cuba's most important industry after sugar during the pre-revolutionary period, its subsequent behavior is still another useful economic indicator of the probable trend of GNP. On the average, the tobacco industry, which produced tobacco leaf, pipe tobacco, cigars, and cigarettes, accounted for about 7 percent of Cuban national income during the post-war period.[40] It was also Cuba's second biggest earner of foreign exchange and employed

38. See his article in *Cuba Socialista,* March, 1966, p. 3.
39. For corroboration on these points, see E. Boorstein's authoritative *Economic Transformation of Cuba* (New York: Monthly Review, 1968).
40. P. S. Stevens, *Cuba: Economic and Commercial Conditions in Cuba* (London: Her Majesty's Stationery Office, 1954), p. 105.

about 130,000 workers in 1953, bettered only by the sugar industry which had, at this time 484,777 workers.[41] It went through a crisis which began in the second half of 1959 and the first half of 1960. The value of exports declined from 79.8 (million pesos) in 1958 to 69.8 in 1959, 54 in 1960, 32.7 in 1961 and 33.1 in 1962. The sharp drop in exports was attributed by our informant to a decline in the quantity and quality of tobacco products.[42] Indeed, the crisis suffered by the tobacco industry was a contributing cause of the 1966 organizational reform, one of whose features was the vertical and horizontal integration of all the various tobacco concerns into one tobacco combine and the use of direct contacts among the latter and its suppliers and customers within the framework of materials allocation.[43] Other official data, fragmentary and somewhat vague, lead to a similar suspicion of a decline in 1960. *Granma* released the following statistics on cement:

. . . imports of cement hit a record high of 258,000 tons in 1955. Following the triumph of the Revolution [the overthrow of Batista on January 1, 1959?] This figure dropped drastically, with the exception of one year [1959?]. Later, it began to rise slowly [1962?], reaching 17,000 in 1963; 33,000 in 1964; 30,000 in 1965 and around 140,000 in 1966.[44]

It added that domestic production continued at 750,000 metric tons since 1959. And "this year's [1967] production set at 875,000 is expected to rise to 950,000 by 1968 and 1,450,000 by 1969." Since cement is an important input in construction, the data above support a finding of the Cuban Economic Research Project that "during 1960, the value [of

41 Ibid., pp. 51, 110.
42. Evelio Lugo, "La industria del tabaco torcido y sus perspectivas," *Cuba Socialista*, May, 1963.
43. Osvaldo Dorticós Torrado, "Avances institucionales de la Revolución," *Cuba Socialista*, January, 1966, pp. 8–11.
44. *Granma*, May 21, 1967, p. 12.

construction] continued its vertical drop."[45] The drop in construction activity was due in large part to several policies taken in 1959 and 1960: the rent law of March 1959 which reduced rents by 30 to 50 percent; the law of vacant lots of April, 1959, which obliged owners to sell to potential constructors at government imposed prices; and the Urban Reform Law of October 1960 which empowered the state to take over mortgages on private and urban dwellings. All of these measures paralyzed private construction and discouraged the maintenance of dwellings and buildings. The government embarked on an ambitious program of construction of rural and urban housing but was unable to surpass pre-1959 levels. In regard to the transport industry, a functionary released the following statistics: he reported the "paralysis of 1,422 buses," and added that similar problems obtained in the railroad, shipping, and merchant marine industries, concluding that "there was almost a total depletion of transport equipment from the capitalist period."[46] He blamed this on the severe lack of spare parts which reached crisis proportions in early 1963.[47] The performance of other industrial sectors seems to have resembled the pattern showed by the several industries described above. The main reason is that the massive transplantation of "complete" factories expected from the Soviet Union and Czechoslovakia from 1960 through 1962 did not materialize to the same extent; this was partially due to the large inefficiencies of the new import-substituting industrialization in toothbrushes, brushes, nuts and bolts, barbed wire, soldering, spades, and other such

45. See its *Labor Conditions in Communist Cuba* (University of Miami, 1963), p. 29; Boris Goldenberg, *The Cuban Revolution and Latin America* (New York: Praeger) p. 257.

46. Omar Fernández "Los problemas del transporte nacional," *Cuba Socialista*, March, 1963, pp. 43, 47.

47. For an impressionistic feel for "the national crisis in spare parts," see *El Mundo*, March 12 and 13, 1963.

articles. The costly imported inputs reached prohibitive levels and emptied foreign-exchange coffers.[48]

Dysfunctional Output

Our ordinal ranking or estimates of Cuban national income of the past decade is suggested further by qualitative data on what may be called dysfunctional outputs. These are "goods" produced which are below their expected use-value, being sometimes of negative value. Under this heading may be classified unwanted inventories, low quality goods, and articles unwanted by either industrial consumers or final users. The tendency to generate such outputs is a fact observed in centrally administered systems. This systemic dysfunction seems to have been pronounced in the first few years of socialism in Cuba and its total magnitude ought to be subtracted to arrive at a more accurate approximation of national income. Unfortunately, the limitations of available data and techniques make it impracticable to calculate this magnitude. We shall only note its substantiality in the Cuban experience. The behavioral paradox of producing unwanted outputs in a planning system relying chiefly on mere physical units was produced in Cuba in the capital and consumer goods areas. We have, of course, no exact quantitative measure of these, but President Dorticós was alarmed by it: "The inventories of the nation appear to be growing at an alarming rate." He complained of the "enormous quantity of iron that waits for the Greek calends in warehouses that cost foreign exchange but have no use to our economy . . ."[49] The Cubans recognized the paradox in this, since everyone knew there was a widespread shortage of capital inputs, yet the Cuban alloca-

48. See Guevara, "Tareas industriales . . .", *Cuba Socialista,* March, 1962, p. 33 *et passim.*
49. Dorticós, "Tareas importantes . . ." *Cuba Socialista,* March 1966, p. 37.

tional system abounded in many such paradoxes. In the light industries field, which produces consumer goods, an official complained that excess capacity had run up to an annual sum of $84,645,500.[50]

The over-all excess accumulation of inventories may have been partially due to a disequilibrium pricing system but it was also due to a negative change in quality. In fact there was a widespread and serious lowering of the quality of consumer goods which ought to be reflected in GNP statistics but which imperfect knowledge prevents us from calculating adequately. "During these years," according to an official of the Ministry of Industries, "there was a decline in the appearance, manufacture and design of a large number of products . . ." This was partially due to "the initial emphasis on the increase of production alone."[51] In late 1965 a number of consumer goods now failed to satisfy the tastes of the sophisticated Cuban housewife, and she refused to buy. Early in 1965 through late August, inventories in women's and children's leather shoes more than doubled; and dress inventories accumulated excessively. A functionary blamed the mounting inventories of shoddy goods on a systemic property: the success indicators imposed on the Cuban enterprise. "The goals are fixed only in [physical] quantities— physical units, gross production, cost per peso of production and tend to hide the economic reason [for production]."[52]

A famous case was shoes. The order to minimize costs per unit was fulfilled (from 85 to 70 cents) by skimping on internal lining and thread reducing the average life of shoes from twelve to three months.[53]

50. Juan M. Castiñeiras, "La industria ligera en la etapa actual," *Cuba Socialista*, June, 1964, p. 4.

51. Ibid., p. 5.

52. "Notas económicas," *Cuba Socialista*, January, 1966, pp. 127–28.

53. Ibid., p. 128.

Boris Pesek notes that (negative) dysfunctional output may be listed as positive; this is more likely in a centrally administered context.

> Suppose that a refrigerator-producer, facing an increased demand for spare parts, is planning to increase the output of spare parts. Suppose further that he is ordered to use his resources to produce an additional number of finished refrigerators. From the standpoint of rational-income accounts, this change will be of no consequence . . . . But the real result of the increased output of finished refrigerators is a decrease in the true national income . . . . The decrease is a multiple of the value because each new refrigerator contains parts that could keep many older refrigerators operational . . . . This shortcoming of the national-income accounting method is of small consequence in a market-directed economy: there a demand for spare parts automatically brings forth a supply of spare parts. [This is not so] given the notorious shortages of spare parts registered in all countries of the Soviet bloc . . .[54]

The argument advanced by Pesek would be invalidated to the extent that there were inflows of precious imported materials, spare parts, technicians, and other needed supplies. Support in these areas did indeed come from the East-bloc countries, and were it not for this aid the Cuban socialist experiment may not have been viable—so much has been implied in the statement of the Cuban policymakers. However, the inflows of supplies from abroad were not in sufficient quantities as to fully replace supplies from the United States and the massive loss of technicians and professionals. Also, the argument advanced by Pesek would operate in other circumstances connected with the administrative mechanism's tendency to heighten the presence of sellers' markets and to inhibit the substitution of one input for another. Let us recall that in an administrative system the firm's input plan is given

54. Boris P. Pesek, *Gross National Product of Czechoslovakia* (Chicago: University of Chicago Press, 1965), pp. 55–56.

by a system of norms and rationed by centralized allocation. That the organizational inefficiencies both in labor allocation and enterprise management rose to a point of intolerability is implied in the planners' justification of the major reorganizational reforms of late 1965 and early 1966. Its major feature was the elimination of unnecessary intermediaries and the provision of greater direct contacts between producers and users to enhance the articulation and specification of product assortments inside the framework of centralized materials allocation. This was clear from one of the major authors of that reform, President Dorticós,

". . . we ought daily to draw production ever close to distribution and to consumption; we ought to produce useful goods and not useless goods." [55]

Hypothesis on National Income

I should now like to state a tentative hypothesis which emerges from this analysis. We are concerned only with the relative movement of Cuban national income, not in its actual levels. The needed details for the latter simply do not exist. In hypothesizing the probable path of national income in the past eleven years I rely heavily on Prime Minister Castro's and JUCEPLAN's later statements on overall production and the serious work on Cuban agricultural production done by the United States Department of Agriculture. But I rely also on the partial data cited on a few main products including the loss of skilled persons and dysfunctional output, and the authority of René Dumont. My tentative hypothesis, moreover, is stated in the less compromising language of rela-

55. From his article "Tareas importantes de nuestros organismos económicos," *Cuba Socialista*, March, 1966, p. 35. See also his "Avances institucionales de la revolución," *Cuba Socialista*, January, 1966. Dorticós heads the Economic Commission of the Central Committee of the Cuban Communist Party.

tive ordinal sizes of a given year's national income in comparison to the year preceding it.

Cuban real national income rose in 1959 well above the previous year's but it declined in 1960—the first year of the socialist experiment. The negative change continued in 1961 and brought it well below the 1958 level; the decline in 1962 was the most rapid and continued at a reduced speed in 1963 when national income reached its nadir. National income rose slightly in 1964 and continued to do so at a higher rate in 1965. A set-back was recorded in 1966 but it increased moderately in 1967 only to decline slightly in 1968. The United States Department of Agriculture studies gave a favorable outlook for 1969 based on partial statistics then available. But in 1970, despite a massive mobilization of voluntary and conscripted labor and an investment rate of 31 percent since 1968 [56] the results in terms of overall GNP seemed poor. In spite of a record sugar harvest of eight-and-half million tons, Castro painted a bleak picture of reverses in many other sectors of production and noted "an increase in our difficulties." [57]

At this point we might note an observation from the growth performance of the Cuban mode of development in its first eleven years, which contradicts one made by Professor Leibenstein. He claimed in a celebrated essay that the net marginal gains from current reallocation of resources by improving the price system are negligible.[58] Cuban experience seems to point to a lesson which clashes violently with this conventional wisdom. That experience shows that departures from current optimal allocation such as the ones amply described in Castro's famous and candid speech of July 26, 1970,

56. Huberman and Sweezy, *Socialism in Cuba*, p. 107.

57. See his famous July 26, 1970, speech, *Granma*, August 2, 1970.

58. Harvey Leibenstein, "Allocative Efficiency vs. 'X-Efficiency'" *American Economic Review*, June, 1966, p. 397.

can lower the long-term growth rate significantly. In other contexts in Latin America and elsewhere, it is now increasingly realized that large long-term losses in GNP can result from the inefficiency of higher duties on finishing-end products and lower duties on earlier-stages manufactures, an inefficiency which can be reversed by uniform taxes charged on the difference between a firm's selling price and cost of materials, and its refund on exports.

In terms of the original purpose for embarking on this study of Cuban material performance—the net efficiency of moral incentives and administrative planning—what can we conclude? We seem forced to admit indeterminacy since, as was mentioned at the beginning of this inquiry, there were other important causes of the decline of Cuban efficiency and per capita income, the most important of which is the low level of technical resources. We can leave our inquiry at that if we like, but it seems possible to proceed by way of a helpful assumption: If moral incentives, and the nonmarket system as a whole, were efficient in terms of ultimate material products, GNP in the first decade ought to have at least been higher in the socialist decade than it was in the preceding market-oriented decade. In terms of moral incentives, Cuban officials date its workable institutionalization by late 1965; yet the growth rate fails to show a self-sustaining upward trend from 1965 to 1970. Let us look at the material performance of the highly imperfect market capitalist system from 1950 to 1959.

National income, in its sense of GNP exclusive of depreciation allowances and indirect taxes, did not decline in the 1950–1959 pre-socialist period even when measured on a per capita basis in 1953 pesos. We cannot say as much of the 1960–1970 record. Indeed, it is hard to read through René Dumont's most recent field research in Cuba without suspecting the possibility of a lower level of GNP in 1970, as compared to, say, 1959.[59] Per capita consumption seems to have increased for the lowest income group, but at the expense of the majority. However, there is an alternative way of viewing growth—from the point of view of productive potential. Here, the Cuban record since 1965 is impressive; social overhead capital, particularly education in badly needed technical skills, has accumulated rapidly. By early 1968, Cuban officials claimed that about one-fourth of the total population was enrolled in one kind of school or another.[60]

TABLE IV

National Income and Related Data *

Year	National Monetary Income (Millions of Pesos)	Population in Thousands	Per Capita Monetary Income	Estimated Purchasing Power of Money (1953–100)	Net Savings as % of Income ‡	Inventories of All Kinds
1950	1,692.0	5,570	304	108.5	6.6	188.5
1951	1,445.6	5,652	344	97.8	9.1	212.2
1952	2,007.1	5,734	350	97.8	15.5	216.2
1953	1,794.4	5,815	309	100.0	4.0	160.7
1954	1,808.2	5,896	307	105.8	11.8	163.7
1955	1,856.3	5,975	311	108.1	11.4	210.7
1956	2,014.5	6,053	333	108.1	12.4	244.5
1957	2,293.7	6,130	374	102.5	15.1	273.6
1958	2,209.6	6,206	356	98.6	13.5	265.3
1959	2,320.08 †	6,336	366	—	—	—

* Source: The 1950–1958 data are from *Memorias* (*Yearbook*) *del Banco Nacional de Cuba*, Ministerio de Hacienda de Cuba.

† Mine on the basis of Dr. Pazos' estimate of a 5% growth and a population growth rate of 2.1% which held at this time.

‡ *Memoria del Banco Nacional de Cuba 1958–59*, Havana, August 30, 1960.

59. René Dumont, *Cuba: Est-Il Socialiste?* (Paris: Editions du Seuil, 1970).

60. *Cuba Economic News* (Havana), Vol. 4, No. 30, 1968, p. 7.

Let us bear in mind, too, that a very high degree of income inequality was drastically reduced with the heavy reliance on moral incentives and administrative allocation—an efficiency criterion the reader may wish to combine with our material yardstick to give him a broader perspective.

CHAPTER FIVE

Historical Viability of Moral Incentives

From Socialism to Communism

Fidel Castro's extraordinary speech to the nation on July 26, 1970 and René Dumont's equally remarkable and most recent field report cast doubts on the viability of the decentralist aspect of the Cuban nonmarket planning system. Both extremely knowledgeable sources drew a bleak picture eleven years after the installment of socialism in Cuba. The early repeated promises of a rapid rise in consumer goods has not come about. Worker discontent seems to have risen as a result as witness the recent high rates of absenteeism and loafing in July and August this year, and against which stronger legal measures have been subsequently taken.[1] The long-term trend seems to be in the direction of greater reliance on the administrative centralist aspect of labor allocation: use of conscripts, physical assignment, legal punishment and cther semi-military methods which have led Dumont to question even the socialist character of Cuban society. Yet, in spite of Dumont's doubts, Cuban socialism has become a communism of some kind. By this latter phrase I mean that the

1. See the draft law against indolence, *Granma*, September 20, 1970, p. 2.

major sector of Cuban productive organization is run along a variant of the communist allocative-ownership rule. In the preface I stated why the allocative versus ownership distinction is invalid, for the character of the various rules according to how a resource is to be used determines the effective nature of its ownership. A high point in the entry into this austere kind of communism was the complete nationalization of the remaining small merchant-business class in the non-agricultural sector in early 1968. That inseparable companion of the market, money, has lost its meaning—as a commanding power over resources, including people. The management of productive resources is done in purely physical terms. Labor is recruited by a strong appeal to contribute its best abilities wherever it is socially needed and by direct allocation; and most consumer goods are rationed according to some austere criterion of need. The sphere of moneyless, "free" distribution of consumer goods has been expanded. The latter trend became pronounced in early 1967 when the Prime Minister declared his support of the program to abolish money as quickly as possible. Earlier he had attacked other market categories such as rent and interest. Concerning money, he said "Money is a vile intermediary between man and the product of his labor . . . . We should not collect any interest because that is capitalistic . . . . [and] replace money by direct distribution and make it less and less important." Shortly after, in mid-July, water and local telephone services were declared to be free of charge.[2] This was in addition to consumption items such as education, medical services, day nurseries, sports events, funerals, certain beauty parlor services, and housing which were distributed free of charge. Residential housing built since 1965 is also allocated in the same manner and rent was scheduled to disappear completely in 1970.* In regard to rationing at nominal money prices, there was a preference for it over distribution through the price system since the former

2. *Granma*, May 28, July 16 and 23, 1967.
* A promise that could not be kept.

was held more in keeping with the communist principle of equity or needfulness in the distribution of consumer goods. This was recently brought out in the case of sugar. At its low fixed price, consumers tended to waste it as feed for pigs and chickens. Instead of raising its price to discourage this, sugar was put back on the ration booklet, this in spite of an average consumption of six-and-a-half-pounds a month per person; this figure was higher than its United States counterpart.[3] The Cuban journals and the press do not mention a probable return to the use of the price system in distributing consumer goods; changes in this sphere will likely take the form of liberalizing quotas listed in the ration booklets or removal of goods in plentiful amounts from the booklet and its distribution at the same fixed price. As in the heavy use of moral prizes for work offered, consumer rationing may be viewed as an attempt to implement the principle of "to each according to his need" although at an austere level. Moral prizes for effort, of course, implements "from each according to his ability" as well.

State ownership is virtually complete in the nonagricultural sector including retail trade; and private farming has by now very little of its usual content. Reforms in March and April of 1968 dealt the final blow to the private sector outside agriculture. This last great wave of nationalizations absorbed more than fifty-six thousand small shops and establishments—bars, nightclubs, restaurants, beauty parlors, bakeries—into the state sector.[4] In agriculture most means of production are, as we know, in the form of state farms—the highest form of state property in the Marxist lexicon. Roughly 30 percent of agricultural lands is allegedly in the hands of small private farmers. Yet if private property is a bundle of powers over the use of property, including the right to market it, it had disappeared for most of Havana province's private

3. *Granma*, January 12, 1969. p. 5.
4. *Granma*, April 7, 1968, p. 3.

farmers by mid-July, 1967. This was in connection with their participation in the state's plans to develop some seventy-four thousand acres of land surrounding Havana and called the Havana Green Belt Program.[5] Private farmers were persuaded to turn over all marketable produce to the state's collection agencies; in return, the state provided free of charge investment funds, housing, equipment services, labor recruited mostly from voluntary mobilizations and so on— thus adding as well to the number of articles already demonetized. They were also guaranteed a minimum price of four *centavos* for a pound of sugar—the prevalent price since 1964. Now they would pay no sales taxes which often ran as high as 20 percent before 1967. They would also be exempt from taxes of other kinds, acquire pension rights and pay no rentals of any kind.[6] The Green Belt idea of developing lands around a large city (mostly with volunteer labor from the city and incorporating private farmers in the manner just described) is to be extended to other places. In November of that year, the Association of Small Farmers vowed to eliminate free market sales altogether, thus implementing the new policy of "withdrawing private farm products from mercantile circulation." Note that this policy reversed an earlier one based on "the mercantile policy of prices and contracts." A decree of September, 1967 gave the state priority in purchasing the farmer's house, vacant lots, and property that he might otherwise bequeath to his children. The outlook for private farming is that of its increasingly being either formally or informally socialized.

The Isle of Youth as Future Model

On the Isle of Pines, now called the "Isle of Youth," there is no question that "the first vanguard of communism

5. *Cuba Economic News* (Havana), Vol. 4, No. 32, 1968, p. 4.
6. *Granma*, January 14, 1968, p. 3; June 23, 1968, p. 8.

in Cuba" has been built no matter how austerely. There, moral stimulation has been more firmly established since most of the working population is made up of volunteers staying on the island for a period of anywhere from several weeks to three years. The island is roughly about the size of Havana province and is located in the Caribbean about sixty miles south of the Cuban mainland. By the latter part of 1969, the island was a well-run commune not unlike its Chinese counterparts. Handed over to the Young Communist League in late 1966, this remarkable social experiment has involved about fifty thousand young Cuban workers (the island originally had a population of eight thousand) involved with a variety of agricultural and industrial projects. Its perspective plan calls for replacing Israel as the world's leading exporter of citrus by the mid-1970's as well as developing a thriving cattle industry, building a complete network of irrigation dams, and establishing a school and recreation system. A rapid rate of colonization from the mainland is expected to multiply its permanent population many times.

In the distribution of labor, the principle of "from each according to his ability" was implemented in a severe form. In accordance with the highest ideal of moral stimulation in labor allocation, an official observer reported: "Each man makes his daily contribution without watching the clock . . . ." [7] Income differentials are far narrower than on the mainland since volunteer workers merely receive a nominal wage of from 60 to 80 pesos, the variation depending on the worker's number of dependents. A greater number of consumer goods are distributed free of charge and the rest rationed as in the mainland. To the volunteers who live in dormitories, housing, food, clothing, transportation, education, books,

7. *Granma*, August 25, 1968, p. 9; see also its series on the Isle of Youth in August and September. A good field report is José Yglesias, "Cuban Report," *New York Times Magazine*, January 12, 1969.

medical services and so on are distributed "freely" on the basis of the worker's conscientiously realistic estimate of his elementary needs. Thus, no matter how austerely, a kind of "to each according to his needs" is followed. The Isle of Youth is publicly held as a model of future social organization—a kind of commune with large decentralized powers. Although its organizational principles are present on the mainland in less intense forms, a similar experiment, called the San Andrés commune, was started in early 1967 in Pinar del Río.

Similarity With War Communism

We might ask why Guevaraism triumphed decisively in late 1966. We can speculate on several possible explanations. Perhaps the Prime Minister's convictions on the matter did not mature to the point of a compelling force until that date. An alternative speculation points to the great need to boost up morale for the great leap forward in developmental investment in late 1966. This impressive campaign resulted in the acceleration of the national rate of investment from 19 to 20 percent from 1962 to 1965, to about 31 percent in 1968; [8] and it is expected to rise even more in 1969 and 1970. In this view, the incentive consumer goods necessary for the functioning of material incentives are simply not available. Yet another reason, by no means unimportant, is the state of national siege from the United States that the Cuban leaders felt more acutely since the U.S. military intervention in Santo Domingo and in Vietnam. The Cuban leaders have, since late 1959, felt threatened by a hostile United States. The colossus looking down 90 miles from the north in disapproval of Cuba's radical domestic and foreign policies was a threatening image and this threat has been increasingly felt. The elimination of the sugar quota, the total embargo, the Bay of Pigs invasion of April 1961, the missile crisis the following year, the Santo Domingo

8. C. Mesa-Lago, "The Revolutionary Offensive," *Trans-action*, April, 1969, p. 24.

invasion of 1965, and the intensification of American involvement in Vietnam had this progressive threatening effect. In a state of emergency it is the ideological purists and radical militants that take a bold view toward risk, who seem to provide the "real" solutions. The state of siege makes them more acceptable since emergency conditions seem to require bold answers. The overriding goal of saving the revolution required centralization of resources to meet this immediate need; and the climate of imminent danger released ideological motives to work harder for common defense and defeat of the national enemy. Guevara was deeply impressed by the moral and emotional forces thus released. He noted that during the four-day Bay of Pigs state of emergency, industrial output did not decline; bureaucratism with what Guevara called its "jungle of paper and red tape (*maraña de los papeles*)" was reduced, production problems and decisions were solved and made by each individual with remarkable alacrity and initiative, and absenteeism disappeared.[9] The reason, according to him, was the ideological commitment precipitated by the state of emergency and he considered this suggestive of the feasibility of moral stimulation. He urged "that the great mobilizing example of the imperialist aggression be made permanent . . . ." The state of continued threat from the United States and its Latin American allies was the fertile ground which allowed the Cubans' millenarian Marxism to take deep roots. The state of emergency continued through the Dominican crisis and the U.S. bombing of North Vietnam, becoming so intense that many Cuban leaders, including Fidel Castro, publicly asserted the imminence of a violent conflict with the United States and the need to keep Cuban society in a state of partial mobilization.[10] The year 1967 saw the same moral fervor rise, perhaps to a higher pitch; it was militantly called

9. See his "Contra el burocratismo," *Cuba Socialista*, February 1963, pp. 5–7.
10. This is reported by C. M. McClatchy, who revisited Cuba in July, 1967 (*The Progressive*, November, 1967), p. 23.

the Year of Heroic Vietnam and symbolized as well Cuba's leadership of an independent Marxist third force among the less developed nations. Events in the following year reinforced the heavy ideological mood and may even have increased in comparison to the previous year. In February, 1968 the prominent party official Aníbal Escalante and his group were found guilty of treasonable conduct in seeking Soviet pressure against Cuba's policies on voluntary work, moral incentives, and for the group's criticism of Che Guevara.[11] This is related to the official Cuban position enunciated by the Prime Minister some six months later attacking Yugoslavia, defending the Soviet invasion of Czechoslovakia, and criticizing the trend of Soviet allocational reforms:

> We are against all those bourgeois liberal reforms within Czechoslovakia . . . a series of reforms that increasingly tended to accentuate mercantile relations within a socialist society: personal gain, profit, all those things.

> Does this by chance, mean that the Soviet Union is also going to curb certain currents in the field of economy that are in favor of putting increasingly greater emphasis on mercantile relations and on the effects of spontaneity in those relations, and those which have been defending the desirability of the market and the beneficial effect of prices based on that market? Does it mean that the Soviet Union is becoming aware of the need to halt those currents? More than one article in the imperialist press has referred jubilantly to those currents that also exist within the Soviet Union.[12]

In 1970, a radical socialist millenarianism continued to animate much of Cuban society particularly young worker-students. The future of moral stimulation depends crucially on the preservation of national morale and one would think that the present leadership has a strong motive for preserving, and exaggerating, if only unconsciously, the sense of national

11. *Granma*, February 11, 1968, p. 2.
12. *Granma*, August 25, 1968, p. 3.

imminent danger in the minds of the Cuban (and Chinese) people.

At this point, an analogy with Soviet War Communism comes to mind. The same socialist millenarianism and state of national siege surrounded its introduction in the Soviet Union in the summer of 1918 at the outbreak of a very complex civil war ending late in 1920. We might recall that some of the Western Allies intervened and aided the White Russian forces in northern Russia, Siberia and elsewhere, and these tried a trade blockade also of the new Bolshevik state, all of which had its parallel in Cuba. The system was abandoned in favor of the famous "New Economic Policy (NEP)"—the first known case of market socialism, if we exclude the eight-month period between November, 1917 and the summer of 1918. An important cause which led to the abandonment of the NEP was the social discontent particularly acute in agriculture and manifested by the abortive Kronstadt uprising of March, 1921 by rebellious Soviet Navy elements. Aside from political reasons prevailing at the time, this discontent was also heavily due to the severe decline in the Soviet output of goods which brought the new Soviet state to a virtual standstill in 1921. Most sources agree that the decline in the Soviet national product was primarily a policy and organizationally induced crisis in spite of a large allowance given by students of Soviet War Communism to the devastating effects of a world and civil war, respectively.[13] The past and present centrally administered system in Cuba bears some important organizational resemblances to the planning system of War Communism. The latter used the state budgetary system of managing the Soviet enterprise which in effect converted the latter to a government office, and its managers and

13. See Margaret Dewar, *Labor Policy in the USSR, 1917–1928* (New York: Royal Institute of International Affairs, 1956); Maurice Dobb, *Soviet Economic Development Since 1917* (New York: International Publishers, 1948).

workers to government employees; it also relied heavily on the administrative allocations of labor and consumer goods which are organizationally similar to those mechanisms currently used in Cuba in these sectors. The agricultural requisitioning of private agricultural products at nominal prices had their counterparts in Cuba till early 1962; but since mid-1967 in Cuba, private farmers were again gradually enlisted to "sell" all of their marketable agricultural surplus to state procurement agencies. In Cuba, however, most of the peasantry have supported the revolutionary leaders and they have been the chief beneficiaries in stark contrast to Soviet War Communism. The latter's attempt at moneylessness, state budgetary financing of enterprises like a government office, and nonmarket allocation of labor caused a depression and had to be abandoned. Will the Cubans similiarly fail and perhaps retreat into a kind of new policy oriented towards the market?

Market vs Moral Incentives in the Long Run

The question just posed is extremely intriguing; it amounts to the same question as to whether the Cuban and Chinese variants of communism will mellow in the long run. What real historical forces would lead to mellowing, if this is at all inevitable? The relatively small size of the Cuban nation and its consequent heavy reliance on international trade and competition abroad is surely of considerable importance; production and sale of products for highly informed, competitive, and unpredictable buyers' markets abroad will steadily call for market-minded experiments and financial discipline in the product performance of such an organization since it must produce for foreign buyers who are free to shift their patronage to other foreign suppliers. On the export side, the pressure now is not so intense since Cuba exports only a relatively few products, principally sugar,

tobacco, minerals and beef. Yet the Cubans have officially embarked on growth through trade and in the future they may
be forced to devise a means of compromise and learn to live
with the impersonal forces of foreign markets. In countries of
semi-continental proportions, such as the Soviet Union and
China, the pressure to adopt an organizational compromise
oriented toward consumerism is not so intense due to a large
domestic outlet and a variety of tastes that may be able to
absorb the brunt of inefficient investments and goods of low
quality although this argument, too, has its obvious limits. A
rich diversity of climates and natural resources may also
make it possible to embark on an investment strategy heavily
biased in favor of import substitution and self-sufficiency.
Pressure for switching over to a new consumer-oriented system would not be so urgent in the latter countries since
planners have a greater power in selling goods for a large
domestic outlet, particularly under conditions of "sellers'
markets." The domestic demand in Cuba is not as large as the
Soviet Union's or China's and the Cuban planners cannot act
with similar power over a large number of its customers—
its international buyers. For a small, foreign-oriented country
an unmistakable yardstick of efficiency makes its presence
known immediately in the form of declining foreign exchange earnings caused by a resulting reduction in the volume
of exports and falling terms of trade. The Cubans discovered
this, for instance, with respect to sugar and tobacco. Indeed,
the success of Cuba's development drive depends largely on
increases in its foreign exchange earnings. This notion of fore-
gone foreign exchange introduces cost consciousness in the
planners, facilitating the ranking and evaluation of investment
alternatives in a more businesslike, efficient, and quantifiable
manner. Finally, such a country requires greater flexibility at
the periphery in adapting to changing technologies and tastes
in foreign markets. Decentralization of production and investment, as the experience of giant American corporations sug-

gests, may diminish the risks of making the wrong decisions. The forces which pressure the Cuban planners to "marketize" are very strong in Cuba. The comparative data with other centrally planned systems which have introduced market mechanisms in varying degrees suggest this:

TABLE V

Exports and Imports as Percentages of
National Income in 1960

Country	Imports	Exports
Czechoslovakia	14	15
Hungary	17	15
Yugoslavia	14	10
Bulgaria	17	15
Cuba	28.5	34.57

From R. León, "La planificación del comercio exterior," *Cuba Socialista*, December 1963, pp. 2, 7. The entries for Cuba are for the year 1958 and are in relation to GNP. Leon cites the U.N. as his source.

The pressures for introducing markets will be felt much more intensely from the need to be efficient in the use of imported goods which use up very scarce foreign earnings. Unlike exports, many more sectors and branches are affected by Cuba's import-dependent developments.

In view of the data cited showing Cuba's heavy dependence on international trade, it is not surprising that some of the earliest and strongest calls for reform and experimentation with the "new models of planning and enterprise management" came from administrators in the Ministry of Foreign trade. For example, in December, 1963 a foreign trade official underscored the need for value planning and criticized planning in mere physical terms.[14] The foreign trade officials

14. R. León, "La planificación del comercio exterior," *Cuba Socialista*, December, 1963, pp. 2, 7.

TABLE VI

Imported Inputs as Percentages of
Total Inputs, 1962

Sector and Branch	Percentage
Mining	40
Metallurgy	44
Construction Materials	11
Petroleum	79
Chemicals	58
Textiles	22
Sugar	4
Food	8
Electricity	21
Construction	12
Transport	4
Agriculture	5

Source: R. León, "La planificación . . ." p. 3.
He cites JUCEPLAN as his source.

have consistently endorsed adoption of what they called "economic methods of management" in contrast to what they pejoratively termed "administrative methods." [15] For example, in late 1965, President Dorticós promised those enterprises engaged in foreign trade and which were on *khozraschet*, freedom to sell directly to foreign customers. The following description of the reform introduced at this time in the foreign trade sector suggests liberalization in other aspects of the activity of an enterprise dealing in foreign trade.

Export operations in the hands of the same agency is responsible for acquiring the agricultural product and processing it industrially, permitting strategic considerations of the export trade to influence directly all aspects of activity in this sector.

15. See *Cuba Foreign Trade* (Havana), November–December, 1965.

The same informant added

> ... we stress the importance of that which assigns export trade responsibility to a so-called "domestic economy" agency. This constitutes, experimentally, an exception to the concentration of the state monopoly in foreign trade exclusively within one Ministry . . . . but at the same time the example may be repeated in the future in accordance with the results of posterior studies and discussions. We must welcome this approach. . . .[16]

A good example of such liberalization is the vertically integrated combine known as *Cubatabaco*. It has been given

TABLE VII

Distribution of Exports by Percentages of
Total Annual Value

Product	1959	1960	1961	1962
Sugar and its derivatives	76.9	79.4	85.0	82.9
Minerals	2.5	1.1	1.3	7.2
Tobacco	8.5	10.2	6.4	4.8
Others	12.1	9.3	7.3	5.1
	100.0	100.0	100.0	100.0

Source: R. León "La planificación . . ." p. 8. He cites the Ministry of Foreign Commerce as his source.

powers to purchase its domestic raw materials on its own and to exercise initiative in setting procurement prices for its domestic inputs.

Another market-like experiment was the creation of the Cuban Hardware Import Enterprise (*Ferrimport*)—known in Cuba as an import-wholesale enterprise. In contrast to the old system, this enterprise now combines the activity

16. *Cuba Foreign Trade* (Havana), November–December, 1965, p. 20. (In English)

of importing and distributing directly to its domestic users. It places orders directly in foreign countries in response to orders placed by domestic enterprises. This experiment, it was stated, would be continued.[17]

It seems from the foregoing that what happens in the Cuban foreign sector will be decisive in influencing future organizational evolution. It is not surprising that the most significant changes—(*khozraschet*) in 1964, the Import-Wholesale Enterprise (*Ferrimport*) in late 1965, the *Cuba-tabaco* combine in early 1966—were first introduced in the export and import sectors. For a small country that must export to grow, such institutional compromises to a sophisticated foreign buyers' market seem inevitable. The Cuban foreign sector will bulk large in importance since the new and official developmental policy, the "*via correcta*," is growth through trade (*desarrollo hacia afuera*).[18] If the few experiments just described are increased as a result of the growth in exports, these enterprises would surely feel pressure to order inputs outside constraints set by centralized materials allocation. Their suppliers, in turn, may want the same privileges in order to be unhampered in supplying inputs—and so on in an ever-widening process. Moreover, these *combinados* may be tempted to accept orders abroad with the aim of making profits which in turn might call for a radical reform of prices to reflect relative costs in an approximately objective manner.

Perhaps the most important future influence on the choice of systems is the ideological erosion stemming from the ideological transformation in Eastern Europe. Cuban planning theory will draw vigor (revisionist contamination) from that source. Partly a product of modernization, partly

17. J. de la Fuente, "Ferrimport, An Experience in Cuban Foreign Commerce," *Cuba Foreign Trade*, November–December, 1965, pp. 13–14.

18. C. Romeo, "Acerca del desarrollo económico de Cuba," *Cuba Socialista*, December, 1965, p. 13.

a result of active competition in informed buyers' markets abroad, and partly the result of the spontaneous erosion of ideology, the ideological changes in Eastern Europe seem to have injected additional pragmatism and a more business-like and scientific approach to allocational problems. The market is being reappraised there and it is being conceived as a cybernetic feedback machinery for generating and transmitting allocational information (relative prices) for the comparison of input and output. One corroding doctrine emanating from the Eastern European reforms which may play a key role in Cuba is Liberman's defense of profit-making under socialism. Liberman's defense is well-known: profit making under socialism is a means towards public satisfaction and is pursued merely as a unifying criterion of productive efficiency. It is not the primary source of stimulation for managerial activity whereas it is under capitalism. He distinguishes between the source of profits and how it is spent under socialism and finds that profit-making under socialism is a morally defensible act [19] in contrast to the Cuban (and Chinese) leadership who point to its universal immorality.

The ideological revolution in Eastern Marxism has indeed influenced or infected Cuban thought since the very early years of socialism. Returning to that "grand debate" on the choice of systems in the formative years, let us recall René Dumont's early reminder to the leaders and planners:

> Yugoslavia has demonstrated the possibility of innovating also in the economic sphere, and its decentralization has achieved indisputable successes . . . .
>
> . . . .
>
> It is perfectly feasible . . . to combine the self-management of current decisions with the general orientation of the economy

19. Yevsei Liberman, "Are We Flirting with Capitalism? Profits and 'Profits'," *Soviet Life*, July, 1965.

in the direction of the Plan, by means of the grant of conditional public credits, with a fixed destination.[20]

The new principle of planned management implicit in this passage has been described elsewhere and seems to be the future ideal of the more radical Eastern European reforms: ". . . central planning authorities. . . . influence by indirect measures (in the field of taxation, export premiums, prices, and so forth)."[21] Central planning through the market relies heavily on the use of indirect measures which seek their goals by working with the market. Its aim is to guide the macro-allocational aspects of resource allocation and growth while leaving its micro-allocational aspects to the market. A Yugoslav official clarifies this concept further: "Planning intervention through *direct price dictation* (price fixing, price ceilings, etc.) is *exceptionally* allowed only where the law of supply and demand virtually does not work or cannot work, that is, where there is no or very little competition. . . ."[22] Presumably a large volume of investment would still be centrally predetermined but its micro-allocation is performed on the basis of market criteria. Thus another Eastern European planner endorses the view that the creation and location of new socialist firms and the allocation of investment in general should be directed by market signals.[23] Planners, of course, need not take market prices as final, but may modify them for social considerations and for market imperfections. But

20. René Dumont, *Cuba: Intento de crítica constructiva* (Barcelona: Editorial Nova Terra, 1965), pp. 152–53.

21. Bedrich Levičik, "New System of Planned Control and Management of the National Economy of Czechoslovakia," a paper distributed at a lecture he gave in Berkeley, 1965, p. 13.

22. M. Todorovic, "Some Observations on Planning," *Socialist Thought and Practise: A Yugoslav Quarterly*, January–March, 1965, p. 32.

23. Quoted in George R. Feiwel, *The Economics of a Socialist Enterprise* (New York: F. A. Praeger, 1965), p. 50.

the important thing, according to the various proponents of market socialism, is that a harmonious relationship exist between the prices used in the Plan and those used in the cost and profit calculation of the enterprise. When these conditions are met, central instructions to profit or perish (to select outputs and inputs so as to obtain an excess of output value over input value) will coincide with the Plan's aim. Thus under this system, which Liberman has called socialist planned commodity [market] system, what is good for society is also good for the enterprise—a tenet of "Neoclassical Marxism." In practice the ideal sketch above is imperfectly implemented as in Yugoslavia due to the practice of disequilibrium price fixing, the politico-administrative allocation of certain amounts of investment, and similar interventions. Nevertheless, the conceptual model described above provides a standard that policy-makers may want to approximate and use for judging present and future reforms of the planning organization.

The appearance of the neoclassical Marxists in Cuban theoretical journals, though brief, may have partly dislodged powerful ideological blocks to the consideration of the marginal opportunity cost theory of value implied by the theory of mathematical allocational (programming); [24] one of them actually suggested use of the marginal cost-benefit in the setting of prices.[25] Others endorsed the consideration as well of the so-called "new models of socialist planning" whose central message is to urge central policymakers to experiment

24. The name is apropos since this new school of Marxism not only teaches the comparative benefits of markets and profit-making but now accepts the marginal opportunity cost (utility) theory of value. The final solutions column of optimal outputs yields at the same time a row of imputed marginal prices of the inputs. Thus the social function of values (prices) is to help deploy resources to their best uses—given of course an acceptable distribution of money incomes (in a live market).

25. Robert N. Anthony, "Las características del costo" *Nuestra Industria: Revista Económica*, December 1967, p. 59, *et passim*.

more with the market mechanism. The long-run material forces mentioned favor the emergence of intellectual and institutional bearers of an alternative morality. This spirit of the market, or of capitalism if we like, with its greater relative emphasis on the pursuit of private benefits than the community's, is perhaps the greatest source of a counter-morality which threatens the historical stability of the communist and religious ethic of intending society's welfare more than one's own in any act of productive behavior. The latter code of moral behavior often works contrary to a person's private hedonic interests and as many observers believe, it may possibly conflict with a biologically rooted human nature.

But revolutionary moral may wane if the Cuban (or Chinese) government succeeds in its diplomatic objectives with the United States. The re-establishment of normal travel and trade relations will make it harder to preserve the high pitch of morale arising from the sense of imminent national danger from the United States. In the historical long run a higher and more complex national income may tempt the leading planners to delegate the mounting tasks of coordinating supplies and demands for individual products to the market and its companion institutions of material incentives and highly differentiated market wages, enterprise autonomy, and profit-making. A higher national income would also make it easier to provide the fund of material consumption goods on which high differential wages can be spent. But, at the point of achieving higher mass consumption, another great cultural revolution may be unleashed to re-establish moral incentives firmly and to roll back the forces making for an otherwise spontaneous erosion of ideology. The social costs of this massive re-socialization to re-internalize the cultural norms and exemplary models of the system of moral incentives may prove large, as we have reason to suspect strongly in the Chinese example. But a powerful leadership committed to its preservation may still risk unleashing such a campaign. We have again reached the limits of safe prediction in mapping out the future course of the Cuban nonmarket system.

For now what convinces the outside observer of its continued existence in the current period is the main leaders' awesome commitment to promoting the communist distributive principle. These are daily and publicly emphasized and reemphasized to the point of an article of faith. If the proof of the pudding is in the eating, the leadership has indeed behaved consistently with their public vows to intensify the present movement towards communism. In spite of the reverses of 1970, Fidel Castro continues to denounce reliance on what he calls capitalist methods. For the time being the forces making for the adoption of an alternative morality lie submerged underneath a heavy overlay of ideology. If the drive to instill decentralist nonmonetary incentives proves unsuccessful due to unfulfilled promises in raising consumption levels, the tendency in adopting stronger centralist administrative measures will be intensified.

There is still another reason why the Cuban leaders will try to preserve moral stimulation—and if that fails, stronger centralized administration. This is the acceleration of the investment effort since 1966. The increased consumption goods that are required for the establishment of an effective system of material incentives would cut down on investment. This may or may not be advisable, but the leaders are not likely to reduce the investment rate drastically due to their desire to hasten growth. Moreover, in a small country like Cuba, planning in physical terms without the main incentive of money wages and market prices may yet reach a higher level of workability as planning experiences accumulate. The latter argument is double-edged. At an early stage in the developmental process where underemployed labor still exists and overtime voluntary labor can be counted upon at little expense in terms of consumer goods, the commitment to the volume of production overshadows the need for optimal re-

source allocation. Yet part of the failure to achieve the promised increases in national income is due to misallccat on of
resources. The Cuban leaders expect to trigger a take-off into
the realm of ever higher national income in the coming decade
by means of a great spurt in agriculture programmed to rise
at a yearly rate of thirteen percent. This will depend on the
acquisition of techno-managerial skills which so far seems
to be the major cause of the failure to grow as cuickly as
promised. There are no guarantees to most courtries embarked on the road to rapid growth that the large fund of
technical skills required will be acquired, in spite of the presence of a will to develop and other favorable institutions. If
Cuba does succeed in achieving technical maturity and its
consequent beneficial effect on national income, it will be
the first state between the Tropics to do so.

Appendix: Moral Incentives, the Market, and Ethical Choice

Moral versus Market Incentives

In this technical appendix I would like to further explore the relation between moral (nonmonetary) means of achieving given ends on the one hand, and, on the other hand, the monetary means we have come to associate with market societies. Whether or not a system working primarily on nonmonetary incentives is compatible with the use of the labor market depends on our concept of a labor market. There are at least two definitions we can offer of labor allocation by means of a market. The first stretches the concept of labor market to its logical limit: "from each according to his relative private disutility (cost)." Now, this is what is meant by "from each according to his ability,"—a necessary requirement in the ideal definition of the mechanism of nonmonetary ("moral") incentives. Under this view of the possible relation between moral and market incentives, what the latter may do is simply change the worker's attitudes toward work and monetary material rewards. Thus, given two sectors, a high income and low income sector respectively, the institutionalization of a set of nonmonetary prizes causes their relative wages to come closer to equality. In the Cuban and Chinese cases, moral incentives also causes the total wage bill to decline. By causing workers to prefer less leisure now in terms of all other goods, whether expressed in money or not, the new more equal wages are still as effective in *retaining* old workers and *attracting* future ones in the various occupations as before, when wages were less equal. Let us take garbage collection as an example. Its relative monetary attractiveness in terms of other occupations declines. If nonmonetary incentives in garbage collection work at all, its now lower monetary prestige is still sufficient in retaining the same number of needed workers; and as requirements rise over time it is also sufficient in attracting new staff.

The other more practical definition of a labor market is one I prefer. It is also the classical Marxist view of the labor market: market allocation requires the award of monetary (material) means in proportion to the value of the individual's products. It is in this second sense that the primary reliance on moral incentives implies the abolition of the labor market. One who holds the thesis of compatibility between moral and market incentives—no matter what their degree of mixture is—implies that modern labor markets can exist without corrosion from its "companion" institution of money and saleable (private) property, at least in the sphere of consumer goods. This is the other reason why classical Marxists rule out the market in a society truly based on the communist allocative rule. This stand is an axiom of Marxist social psychology connected to the Marxian theory of alienation. In this view of human alienation, that phenomenon is viewed chiefly as a social condition manufactured at this point in history by the rise of market (commodity) production and its companion institutions—notably the labor market, where human labor is sold like any other commodity. The market theory of alienation is an old one and is found in Deuteronomy in the diatribes there against money and money-making. While its roots are in the Bible, the market theory of alienation has since been developed into a more systematic social theory. Its earliest modern collectivist version is Thomas

More's *Utopia* (1516) and Gerard Winstanley's *The Law of Freedom* (1652). In this liberal and socialist view, man is basically good, or at least not basically bad, and what makes him bad is chiefly his social environment. The market imposes evil and artificial values and behavior—the competition for individual material gain, for instance. This view of human nature is still popular today among socialists, literary and radical humanists and religious leaders. Even Adam Smith wrote in his classic *Wealth of Nations* that a market participant "intends . . . only his own gain." This drew profound indignation from the young Marx of the *Economic and Philosophical Manuscripts* (1844): "the only moving forces which political economy recognizes are the lust for gain . . . and . . . competition." This is defined as evil behavior in the Marxian theory of alienation; society *ought to be* made up of community-centered and loving individuals, and only under nonmarket institutions can this be brought about. I propose to examine this foundational doctrine of the radical opponents of the market system since it is by no means obvious, and the alternative to the market might be worse from the point of view of another ethical theory of man and society.*

I shall make use of the three-dimensional graph of applied ethical analysis, or of the theory of moral choice. The third dimension is represented as altitude contour curves and stand for ever higher levels of moral satisfaction (utility). The first and second dimensions (axes) represent any two things from which a moral choice has to be made. Although this extremely valuable graph is borrowed from the general theory of taste-maximization under conditions of scarcity, I shall not make a distinction between mere preference and moral choice. Suffice it to say that in general analysis the distinction between the two seems untenable since my choice now in buying butter competes with one ordinarily regarded as moral: giving the same amount to poverty- or war-stricken persons. Each pref-

* *E.g.*, the Yugoslav theory of alienation which asserts it is worse under administrative socialism than in either capitalism or market socialism.

erence act is thus morally tainted. Our discussion, so far, pertains to the demand side; let us now discuss this third-dimensional graph from the technology or supply side—again, under conditions of scarcity. From the technology side, an altitude line represents a level of the possible, and its slope indicates a constant capacity to transform the object measured on the horizontal axis into the desired object measured on the vertical axis. The other shape in which the possibilities indicator comes is the altitude contour that curves downward, the slope of which indicates a diminishing capacity to transform one object into the other. We shall use both shapes.

We are now ready to describe a model of decentralized behavior which includes market behavior as one specific instance; but our model could also represent the behavior of a person acting on the basis of moral incentives. It seems reasonable to represent a market as any situation where agents determine their allocative activity with the help of known prices (or costs). The particular way in which prices are set is irrelevant to this definition; they may be set by imperfectly competitive forces or by central planners. Is a market participant capable of community-centered behavior? The model below helps us in stating the conditions under which civic-minded behavior occurs. It has the property of being statistically specifiable and of being measurable.

We measure a given person's total income, including his leisure measured at its opportunity cost, on the horizontal axis and it increases from A to B to C during the period being considered. Another person's—it can be a geographic location[1]—corresponding real income is measured on the vertical

---

1. In this case the real income of a place or community might be measured on a per capita basis; this measure might be taken by a potential contributor as providing a picture of the representative individual of a place deserving aid or contributions. Measurement in per capita terms allows us to scale down the total income of a place for analytical manageability and the qualification allows us to retain

Other's Income

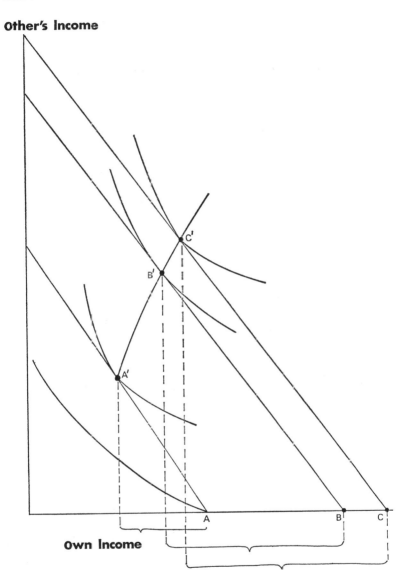

our one-to-one terms of transfer in the model; if I give up $100, this
does not mean, for our purposes, that I give each of my neighbors
$100 divided by the population of the neighborhood.

axis and the income constraint line is sloped at forty-five degrees to indicate a one-to-one terms of transfer or exchange. Our particular example's objective function or moral utility ordering of the final value to him of his neighbor's real income—which might be equated to the same other person's utility—shows desire on his part to contribute part of his income, including leisure, to the other if the former's income is initially at A. This "act of benevolence" shifts him to a higher moral indifference contour at A′ and the size of his voluntary contributions is measured by the curly bracket from A to A′. It seems clear from the model that benevolent behavior is compatible with "self-interest" or "selfishness." These terms simply mean in the context of decentralized allocative activity including market behavior "doing one's own thing," or being self-motivated in enhancing one's own goals—whatever these are. What makes the representation above of general decentralized action a market situation, is the taking of an act with the aid of a known list of the costs of each action. The locus of optimal points trace out a benevolence curve but let us call it a voluntary contributions curve so-named after the nature of the immediate end sought. Note that it depends on other factors as well than on mere levels of affluence. An affluent person with vertically biased moral ordering contours would give little or none of his goods and labor to others; if the curves bend in a northeasterly direction our example would even show envy. The size of contributions depends on the flatness of his moral utility contours and as a hypothesis, it would seem to depend a great deal on cultural inheritance and level of self-awareness. The diagram above clarifies a charge often made by radicals and conservatives alike that markets always mean the sway of monetary selfish interest.[2] Professor Boulding's recent article

2. That this assumption may often lead to error in human relations is shown in my note "Why It Is Cheap, Not Dear, To Marry A Ph.D.", *Journal of Political Economy*, September–October, 1969.

on the subject titled "Economics as a Moral Science" charged that discipline with neglect of ethical behavior or moral stimulation which he sees in acts of benevolence to other persons; this neglect is attributed by him to an alleged assumption of the standard models of efficiency and exchange of universal selfishness. He defines "Selfishness . . . [as] the independence of indifference functions, such that it makes no difference to me whether I perceive you as either better off or worse off." [3] He suggests that the bias for assuming selfishness —in Boulding's sense—in the standard approach is the difficulty of incorporating the effects of another persons' utility on one's utility function. Boulding's charge seems to be extreme in view of our analysis; another person's utility can be incorporated into one's utility function as shown above by taking the other person's real total income as an index of his utility.

With regard to the decision to work, we can show the effect of moral stimulation or incentives on the worker with the aid of a similar diagram. The variables on our horizontal and vertical axes would be leisure hours and money wages per hour, respectively. The altitude contours represent his levels of satisfaction and private valuation of leisure in terms of money. Moral stimulation flattens out these curves; in contrast to the old curves the altered ones signify a diminished preference for leisure in terms of money—and therefore shows greater willingness to supply manhours at the same market wages. But a regime relying primarily on moral incentives would want to reduce wages that are unduly high, and the straight line in our imaginary diagram which shows the market exchange rate between money and leisure (the reverse of work hours) becomes less steep. This would ordinarily reduce manhours supplied, but due to the new work ethic, our imaginary diagram shows it does not. Here, again, we have shown the theoretical complementarity between moral and

3. K. E. Boulding, in *American Economic Review*, March, 1969.

market incentives; as a matter of fact, this is the way they co-exist in capitalist market societies. However, the mixture between moral and material incentives in modern market societies is likely to be so favorable to private material incentives as to be unacceptable to the egalitarian socialist. It would seem that a country relying primarily on moral incentives would desire such a high mixture in favor of moral incentives as to make it incompatible with the labor market.

I single out the labor market because a system working primarily on the basis of moral incentives is compatible with a consumer goods market. Thus, given a lump-sum money income divided according to some criterion of equity, spending it on the consumer goods market would ensure distribution according to need. Classical Marxism of the type dominant in Cuba seems to extend the meaning of moral incentives to imply the abolition of all markets and of money as command over goods. But it is not strictly implied by the communist allocative rule.

Money wages are paid in Cuba and show a graduated range comparable to, say, wages in Czechoslovakia in the mid-1960's. These wages could possibly roughly reflect the new private relative costs after moral stimulation was actively applied to the labor market. The labor market, however, does not exist in Cuba in spite of the fact that wages are still paid. For one thing, labor allocation is done chiefly by a combination of moral incentives and centralized assignment. The wages paid are really pseudo-wages of a nonmarket character. The labor market concept requires the existence of a consumer goods market (the reverse is untrue). In Cuba, however, most consumer goods are distributed to the citizenry and workers not through the market but through egalitarian physical distribution. By the latter I mean physical rationing and subsidized services including free, moneyless distribution of goods. The same is true in regard to labor distribution and consumer allocation in China although consumer rationing is practiced on a lesser scale.[4] Insofar as this is the case, the latter practices moral incentives in a more imperfect form— by giving greater scope to market incentives in labor recruitment.

With respect to the behavior of the agent known as the firm the objective function described has applications. Thus market socialist and capitalist firms need not single-mindedly maximize profits nor must their managers, as witness the techno-manager in the United States whose salary is somewhat independent of profits. That assumption of standard theory is an oversimplification for predicting price-output adjustments of the average firm in strongly competitive and atomistic situations but never meant as a psychological description of motivation. Obviously, firms have to make a minimum profit below which is "disaster" but profits above that level may be given up for another objective such as autonomy or security. But whether firms maximize or just make profits or whether they are primarily stimulated to produce for the sake of profits has to be shown quantitatively for every system at each particular historical period. Some of Professor Liberman's admirers in Cuba who, from 1960 to 1965, favored the adoption of an alternative socialist system with strong market characteristics believed that the efficiency motive for making profits in contrast to making or maximizing profits for material motives could be divorced from each

4. Although Vogel and Richman do not explicitly say so, the impression they give is that labor is chiefly allocated by moral incentives and by administrative authorities. See their works cited in chapter two. This is also the impression I get from C. S. Chen (translated by C. P. Ridley), *Rural People's Communes in Lien-Chiang* (Stanford: Hoover Institution Press, 1968). The latter author stresses the administrative role in labor allocation of commune authorities while Vogel mentions the role of a national assignment system and the strong role of the local labor bureau.

other. Charles Bettelheim argued thus in his articles published by the Cuban journals. For profits to play the role of a comprehensive (synthetic) efficiency criterion, he stressed that the former ought to be founded on a pricing system that reflected the social utility of products including factors such as capital.[5] His variant of "market socialism," which he defended in his grand debate with Dr. Guevara in early 1964 and reiterated in late 1966 in the Cuban journals, harped on the point that profits could be desired solely for providing a test of overall efficiency and not for material reasons and thus profit-sharing of the kind envisioned in the latest Liberman proposals need not be introduced. Our previous model shows the plausibility of his scheme. Yet Cuba is a low income country and the use of markets and profits is likely to play the role of a Trojan horse for the spirit of capitalism—material stimulation—to emerge. In a poor country the efficiency criterion of profits may have to be accompanied by a bonus or profit-sharing scheme else managers and workers may not be stimulated enough to fulfill that goal. The Cuban policymakers who wish to increase the scope of all forms of material incentives as well as other market institutions face two kinds of choices. The technical choice is to weigh the value to them of GNP lost as a result of eliminating material incentives or a market institution and replacing it with a particular institution within the system of moral stimulation. Should the opportunity cost of this be excessive they may wish to re-set the present level of moral incentives and nonmarket methods used. The second choice is ethical and substantive because it calls for the re-evaluation of the doctrine which views material stimulation as psychologically immoral or "alienating." A mark of the "New Marxism" in Eastern Europe is its vindication of the latter under the rubric of "personal produc-

5. His latest article on the subject appeared in *Nuestra Industria: Revista Económica*, December, 1966, p. 36, *et passim.*

tion," "personal interest," or Liberman's "profits" (in quotes)
as an "objective category"—and thus a main goal of socialism.[6]

Is Moral Stimulation Good?

The operation of the mechanism of moral incentives suggests a purely internal drive towards the performance of a
voluntary activity without external prodding. Moral stimulation, on the other hand, suggests the intervention of an
external agency that institutes moral incentives as social norms
and which seeks to have these internalized by the population.
The socially approved competition for moral titles thereby
acts to enhance group solidarity, a reconciler of potential
conflict among workers who might otherwise differ violently
about what each one was worth in terms of his share of the
national income.

I refrained in this study—except in references not due
to me—from using that confusing word "economics." In
studies of this kind, it is likely to be counter-productive or
misleading. By not using that term, I hope to show its super-
fluity. Standard approaches to the efficiency of productive
organizations, partly as a result of the misidentification of
national production with material things, have unduly
stressed the partial efficiency problem of how social organizations achieve their material goals. Yet social organizations
have more than one class of goals some of which are
commonly referred to as "nonmaterial." It is clear from any
serious understanding of Cuban social reality that its main
leaders possessed other goals they were eager to actualize
which fall under the rather unhappy word, "nonmaterial." To
cite just one relevant example, one of the main goals of the

6. E.g., *Komunist* (Belgrade), August 8, 1963, p. 6; Y. Liberman,
"Are We Flirting With Capitalism? Profits And 'Profits', *Soviet Life*,
July, 1965.

general system of moral stimulation was the pursuit of communist egalitarianism—"from each his ability, to each his need." Moral stimulation was not implemented solely as a mobilizer of effort and skills for a massive investment effort but as a social invention to replace the old socio-moral norms inherited from the past. That egalitarianism was valued greatly by the leaders is shown in their early hasty efforts at eliminating overt unemployment quickly; by their policy of reallocating resources in favor of the countryside; by the extension of opportunities to racial minorities, women, and children. Egalitarianism may be considered a nonmaterial output of the Cuban productive system alongside more familiar material outputs such as butter and barbering. The latter are more familiar to the student of productive organizations since they make a more visually dramatic appearance in the world with price and cost tags hung on them, so to speak. Nonmaterial goods which issue from productive organizations are not as easily seen nor measured since no price tags readily accompany their appearance in the productive process. They can, however, be crudely represented or measured on some social index; for example, egalitarianism might be represented by the degree to which income equality is approached. Our previous discussion showed, I hope, that egalitarianism of a high degree was one of the achievements of Cuban productive organization. This was achieved largely by use of the allocational system of moral stimulation.

An objection to the above procedure is that these "nonmaterial" ends are "non-economic." The adjective "economic" however—and "political" for that matter—does not refer directly to the nature of the ends and outputs themselves but to the manner of achieving them. The ends are "economic" only indirectly to the extent that, to quote a treatise on the subject, they "are capable of being stated as ends of consciously husbanded effort . . . ." The author of that treatise quotes L. Robbins' well known statement of the mid-thirties that these goals "may be 'material' or 'immaterial'—if ends can be so described. But if the attainment of one set of ends involves the sacrifice of others, then it has an economic aspect . . . . The habit, prevalent among certain groups of economists of discussing 'economic satisfactions' is alien to the central intention of economic analysis." [7] The habit of speaking of goals as being "economic" or "political" has led to the questionable view that wants are divisible into component parts; for example, it has been partly responsible for an untenable dualistic theory about the existence of a separate field of study called "colonial economics" by its would-be inventor, J. H. Boeke. In this view, "Western analytical economics" is inapplicable to formerly colonial or colonial underdeveloped countries because of its alleged hedonistic doctrine of *homo oeconomicus* whereas needs and wants are restricted and pre-modern in peasant-dominated areas.[8] When a leading member of Cuba's eight-man Political Bureau, Armando Hart, stated that "production . . . is the most important political interest before us at this time . . .",[9] we can interpret this to mean that production was the end and "political" was the manner of achieving it. A related quotation— particularly relevant to this study—has been expressed by an authority on Chinese labor organization: "In a certain sense nonmaterial incentives may be considered outside the scope of economics." [10] From the allocative point of view this is not true, as I hope I have shown in this study of moral incen-

7. Tapas Majumbar, *The Measurement of Utility* (New York: St. Martin's Press, 1958), pp. 14–15.

8. See J. H. Boeke, "The Theory of Indies Economics," and his "Social and Economic Needs," in *Indonesian Economics, The Concept of Dualism in Theory and Policy*, edited by a Group of Dutch Scholars (The Hague: W. van Hoeve, Publishers, Ltd., 1961).

9. *Granma*, Sept. 3, 1967, p. 4.

10. Charles Hoffman, *Work Incentive Practices and Policies In The People's Republic of China, 1953–1965* (New York: State University of New York Press, 1967), p. 58.

tives. Finally, the word "economic" is altogether avoided here to avoid being associated with statements made too casually and erroneously by many writers that "it is only a minor oversimplification to say that the economist's world is one of selfishness and competition . . ." [11]

The reader may ask: Is the Cuban system a good one? Is it better than a possible alternative system? Here we face an impossibility—no answer exists valid for everybody. We require an empirical estimate of the capacity of the two alternative organizations in question to transform social goals into one another. But whose value system shall we use as an efficiency criterion for evaluating the goodness of a productive state in comparison to another? The following diagram illustrates the difficulty of an overall evaluation of efficiency or goodness. Let us take just two social goals: egalitarianism and choice. Let us say, as it seems probable from our study, that the present Cuban productive organization produces much growth in egalitarianism and relatively less of the room for choice than the pre-revolutionary capitalist system. The production possibilities marked I and II, respectively, represent this situation. Superimpose two different sets of ethical rankings of these social goals on the capacities curves just mentioned. The first set of valuational curves may be regarded as those of the Cuban leaders; they are relatively flat and show a strong relative valuation for egalitarianism in terms of choice. The other set of valuational curves may represent a California-type self-actualizer's who prices the room for choice very dearly. Clearly, from the leaders' viewpoint, system I is ethically superior to system II but our self-actualizer would disagree by claiming the opposite view.

We limited our consideration here of trade-offs to choice versus egalitarianism; but for most people, there is also the question of the relative amount of material goods that can be

11. W. T. Tucker, *The Social Context of Economic Behaviour* (New York: Holt, Rinehart and Winston, Inc., 1964), p. 10.

provided by the two systems. Since their abilities to produce material goods differ, our final choice between them depends on our view of the technical objective rate at which goods are sacrificed to enable the system to produce a more egalitarian structure of wages and opportunities for people. Our discussion of Cuban efficiency and growth for the two sets of decades, respectively, suggest similar comparative objective capacities curves as the previous one we drew. The one exception to this statement is that growth in GNP replaces choice. Now assume the same view of the relative importances of the two performance criteria, that is to say, we retain the same shapes of the subjective ranking contours. An egalitarian would give a higher rank to the Cuban nonmarket system. But a believer in the morality of self-interest, or in another

Growth of Egalitarianism

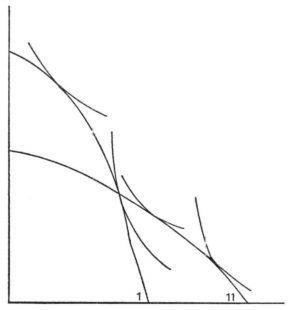

Growth of Choice

morality such as the ethical theory founded on the psycho-biological work of Abraham Maslow,[12] would rank the market as superior. The reader is invited to form his own choice on the basis of the same ethical logic.

12. See his well-known classic, *Toward a Psychology of Being* (Van Nostrand, 1968).

Index